BILLY SUNDAY AND THE REDEMPTION OF URBAN AMERICA

LIBRARY OF RELIGIOUS BIOGRAPHY

available

Billy Sunday and the Redemption of Urban America
  by Lyle W. Dorsett

Liberty of Conscience: Roger Williams in America
  by Edwin S. Gaustad

forthcoming

The Divine Dramatist: George Whitefield and the Rise of
Modern Evangelicalism
  by Harry S. Stout

William Gladstone
  by David Bebbington

Billy Sunday
and the Redemption
of Urban America

Lyle W. Dorsett

WILLIAM B. EERDMANS PUBLISHING COMPANY
GRAND RAPIDS, MICHIGAN

Copyright © 1991 by Wm. B. Eerdmans Publishing Co.
255 Jefferson Ave. S.E., Grand Rapids, Mich. 49503

Printed in the United States of America

Library of Congress Cataloging-in-Publication Data

Dorsett, Lyle W.
   Billy Sunday and the redemption of urban America / by
Lyle W. Dorsett.
      p.   cm.
   Includes bibliographical references.
   ISBN 0-8028-0151-X
   1. Sunday, Billy, 1862 – 1935.   2. Evangelists — United States —
Biography.   3. Baseball players — United States — History.
4. Evangelistic sermons.   5. Sermons, American.   I. Title.
BV3785.S8D67   1990
269'.2'092 — dc20
[B]   90-45906
                                                               CIP

Billy Sunday's sermons *Heaven* and *Get on the Water Wagon* are both
copyrighted by Grace Theological Seminary and are reprinted with
permission.

*This book is
dedicated
with love to my wife,
Mary Hayes Dorsett*

Contents

Foreword, by Nathan O. Hatch   ix

Acknowledgments   xi

Introduction   1

1. Hard Times (1862-1882)   5

2. Onward and Upward (1883-1891)   17

3. The Apprenticeship (1891-1896)   43

4. The Kerosene Circuit (1896-1907)   61

5. The Redemption of Urban America (1908-1920)   85

6. Agony and Decline (1921-1935)   124

7. Legacy   144

   Afterword (1935-1957)   158

84334

CONTENTS

Notes on Sources   161

Appendix   168

    Heaven   169

    Get on the Water Wagon   181

Index   208

Foreword

The history of Christianity in American is punctuated with revivals and revivalists—from George Whitefield to Billy Graham. The recurring presence of such powerful preachers has lent a dynamic character to American Protestantism. In their wake powerful religious movements have churned at the fringes of formal church structures, Christians have continued to experiment with new measures to communicate the gospel, and audiences across a wide range of denominations have been inclined to respond to the revivalist's straightforward and persuasive appeal.

Like Charles Finney and Dwight L. Moody before him, Billy Sunday took up the revivalist's call as a layman. Raised in rural poverty and with little formal education, Sunday moved from small-town Iowa to Chicago in the 1890s in order to play major league baseball. After his conversion, it was his fame as an athlete that first opened doors for him to speak publicly about his Christian beliefs.

With stern and independent conviction, Billy Sunday

barnstormed as an evangelist, spending nearly a decade traveling in small midwestern towns at the turn of the century. As his fame and influence grew, he moved to the nation's urban centers. Opinionated and flamboyant, Sunday preached a gospel that resonated with country phrases, homespun idioms, and blunt, commonsense wisdom. Sunday had the perfect touch for many Americans who found themselves transplanted from rural to urban America.

Lyle Dorsett's fresh biography offers a careful and frank assessment of Billy Sunday and his ministry. Quick to note Sunday's sincerity, dedication, and evangelistic success, Dorsett does not shrink from describing the more troublesome side of his career: how fame, financial success, and political influence worked to corrupt the evangelist and his family. The story of Billy Sunday is laced with contradictory elements: sacrifice and self-delusion, high purpose and triumphalism, identification with the poor and hobnobbing with the rich. The great value of Dorsett's account is his depiction of Billy Sunday as neither hero nor villain. Instead, Dorsett introduces a human figure whose struggle to redeem urban America in God's name involved both achievement and tragedy.

Nathan O. Hatch

Acknowledgments

My greatest debt in writing this book is to my friend and colleague Prof. Mark Noll, professor of history at Wheaton College (Illinois). Mark suggested that I write this book. He also proved to be a wise and insightful critic of both substance and style.

My friend since undergraduate days, Prof. Bruce Clayton, the Harry A. Logan, Sr., Professor of History at Allegheny College, Pennsylvania, has once again read my manuscript and offered invaluable criticisms. An unusually able biographer and historian, Bruce helped me more than I can ever express.

Mary Hayes Dorsett, my wife, sometime coauthor, mother of my children, and best friend, was again an unusually keen critic. This book is much better than it was before she gave me her counsel. She also prepared the index.

Robert Shuster, my colleague, friend, and director of the archives of the Billy Graham Center, Wheaton College, saved me months of time. Paul Ericksen, Lannae Graham, Fran Brocker, and others on Bob's splendid staff gave me endless assistance. And Bob's *Guide to the Microfilm of the Papers of William and Helen Sunday* (1987) is absolutely essential to anyone working on Billy Sunday. More than a guide, it is a thoroughly researched book—an original contribution to knowledge. Without Shuster's staff, archives, and *Guide,* I would still be taking notes for this book.

The Rev. Jerry Root, a friend and fellow author, encouraged me as I did this book. I am particularly grateful to him for giving me Billy Sunday's marked personal copy of E. M. Bounds's book on Satan.

I also thank my friend and fellow historian Prof. Mark S. Foster of the University of Colorado, Denver, for helping me with the baseball history portion of my research. Peg Dietrich, a freelance writer in Denver, former student, and longtime friend, did research on Sunday's Colorado crusades for me.

Evelyn Brace, Diane Garvin, and Ginny Feldmann put various drafts into the word processor.

Grace Theological Seminary of Winona Lake, Indiana, generously gave me permission to quote from Billy Sunday's papers, and in particular to reprint two of the evangelist's sermons. I also want to thank John Lorch, the Grace Seminary security guard who gave me a tour of the Sunday home. I drove to Winona Lake from Wheaton to see the house. The tour guide was away. Lorch opened the house, gave me a tour, and stayed while I examined the Sunday family library.

Not all of my benefactors mentioned here share my theological views or interpretations of history. Nevertheless, they have provided much help, and I am grateful.

Lyle W. Dorsett
Wheaton, Illinois
March 1990

Introduction

For almost a quarter century Billy Sunday was a household name in the United States. Between 1909 when he first made the pages of the *New York Times* and 1935 when that great urban daily covered his death and memorial service in detail, people even marginally informed about current events had heard of the former major league baseball player who was preaching sin and salvation to large crowds all over America. Not everyone who knew of the famous evangelist liked him. Plenty of outspoken critics derided his flamboyant style and criticized his theologically conservative doctrines. But he had hundreds of thousands—perhaps millions—of loyal defenders, and they were just as loud in their praise as the opposition was in its disdain.

Whether people stood for or against the Reverend William A. Sunday, they all agreed that it was difficult to be indifferent toward him. The Iowa-born religious leader was so extraordinarily popular, opinionated, and vocal that indifference was the last thing he would invoke from people. His most ardent admirers were confident that this rural-bred preacher

1

was God's mouthpiece, calling Americans to repentance as Amos had called Israel centuries before. Sunday's critics held that at best he was a well-meaning buffoon whose sermons vulgarized and trivialized the Christian message and at worst he was an outright disgrace to the name of Christ.

There are elements of truth in both of these views. He was often guilty of oversimplifying profound truths, and at times he spoke from gross ignorance rather than a heavenly vantage point. He was also a man with numerous flaws. He certainly overindulged his children, put enormous demands on his wife, sought the applause of the crowd, confused the will of God with his own social and political agenda, placed too much emphasis on money, and equated the gospel of Jesus Christ with special interests and American foreign policy. Nevertheless, Billy Sunday was a sincere man whose life was fundamentally changed by his response to an evangelist's call to repent of his sins, to believe that Jesus Christ died in his place for those sins, and to follow Christ in thanksgiving by worshiping and obeying him. Following this spiritual rebirth, the convert became deeply devoted to Jesus Christ—a devotion manifested in living out many of the teachings of Christ as found in the New Testament's four Gospels. The professional baseball player became a regular churchgoer. He also studied Scripture and became unusually generous toward the needy. Furthermore, Sunday was constrained by an obsession to tell others how he had finally found inner peace and a more purposeful life. At first through lectures and then in sermons, he related how Jesus Christ gave him a new life of meaning, peace, and hope. This same gospel, he said, would similarly transform others. The evidence is overwhelming that it did.

If Billy Sunday was sincere, devoted, and motivated, he was also a product of his times and a conduit of the culture and mores of middle America. On the other hand, the blue-eyed, athletically trim dynamo took many stands against the winds of consensus, and he persuaded multitudes to join him in a war against much of the conventional wisdom of the early twentieth century.

It is true that Sunday was a showman who craved an audience and loved applause. But he also touched the lives of countless men and women of all social classes, helping them escape various forms of personal bondage and find freedom in the gospel of Jesus Christ. And if he did not convert all of urban America to his brand of Christianity, he at least played a major role in helping to keep conservative biblical Christianity alive in this century.

Because several biographies of Billy Sunday have been written, it is incumbent upon me to justify one more. Perhaps it is enough to say that I was invited to do the book. My friend and colleague Prof. Mark Noll told me that as general editor of the Library of Religious Biography for William B. Eerdmans Publishing Company, he wanted me to provide a volume on Billy Sunday. My career-long interest in American urban history and my more recent commitment to Christianity and evangelism conspired to make me a reasonable choice. These personal and professional factors encouraged me to accept this invitation, and it has been all the more attractive because of what I perceive as a need for a modern life of Billy Sunday. It has been nearly three decades since the last biography of Sunday was published. Entitled *The Billy Sunday Story*, this "authorized" (by Mrs. Sunday) biography by Lee Thomas is clearly written and useful, but it suffers from the same uncritical determination to sanctify Sunday as the two "authorized" (by Billy Sunday) biographies that appeared in 1914: Elijah P. Brown's *The Real Billy Sunday* and William T. Ellis's *"Billy Sunday": The Man and His Message*. In 1955 William G. McLoughlin, Jr., published a thoroughly researched, thoughtfully conceived, and well-written book called *Billy Sunday Was His Real Name*. This is still an important study, but any volume over three decades old fails to ask questions that are being raised in these times. Furthermore, as significant as McLoughlin's book is in revealing the inner workings of mass evangelism and the Sunday organization, it does not provide much about Sunday's personality, with all its agonies and insecurities, or about the dynamics of his relationships with his wife, children, or co-workers. Also, for better or worse, I am more sympathetic to Mr. Sunday than McLoughlin was when he wrote his book.

Previous biographers had advantages I cannot share. Both Ellis and Brown knew Billy Sunday personally, and McLoughlin and Thomas benefited from extensive interviews with Mrs. Sunday. Although I cannot boast even an acquaintanceship with any member of the Sunday clan, I did have access to the Sunday family correspondence and papers, which were not available in entirety until after Mrs. Sunday's death in 1957. While newspaper files and the books of others have enriched my version of Sunday's life, my unique contribution lies in having been able to mine these untapped family letters. They relate facts, reveal emotions, discuss problems, and generally shed new light on the Sunday story. My goal has been to utilize these untapped primary sources and fashion a portrait of Billy Sunday that will neither gloss over his faults nor exaggerate his strengths.

In order to show something of the evangelist's style, theology, and mind, I have also included two of Billy Sunday's sermons, reproduced in their entirety. I believe they provide evidence of more polish than his detractors typically credit him with and demonstrate that he was not in fact the buffoon many believe him to have been.

1 Hard Times

1862-1882

"I am of a sensitive nature."

The year Andrew Jackson was elected President of the United States, William Sunday, the man who was to be the evangelist's father, was born in the mountainous wilds of south central Pennsylvania. It was difficult to make a living in the hill country where he grew up, and it was even harder to earn enough money to purchase good farm land in Pennsylvania or neighboring states such as Maryland and Ohio. So, like many young men of Pennsylvania Dutch parentage, William Sunday looked west for economic opportunity. His interest was focused on a place over eight hundred miles away called Iowa. Formed as a territory in 1838, this land, bordered on the west by the Missouri River and on the east by the Mississippi, was reported to have rich soil, rolling hills, and an ample growing season. The territory spanned over three hundred miles between Nebraska and Illinois. It became a state in 1846, and a few years later William Sunday arrived to begin a new life. Working as a contractor, brick mason, and seasonal farm hand, he did some building in Cedar Rapids and then moved to Story County in the center of the state.

Several years before the sturdy Pennsylvanian showed up in Story County, a man named Martin Corey, his wife, and eight children homesteaded there. Having spent three months on the journey from Syracuse in Kosciusko County, Indiana, they arrived in a covered wagon at Story County near Ames in 1848. Life was not easy for the Coreys. Mr. Corey did blacksmithing, made wagon wheels, and built his own house while he cleared his land for crops. His wife and children worked equally hard, making most of their own clothing and furniture and growing their own food.

The Corey's oldest daughter, Mary Jane, had always worked alongside her parents. Though hardened by the chores of milking cows, yoking oxen, harnessing horses, and helping to pull stumps from the opening farmland, she remained an attractive woman, with striking dark eyes, dark hair, shapely features, and a sensitive disposition. William Sunday was impressed with her, and evidently she found the emigrant from Pennsylvania to her liking as well, for the couple was married in the middle 1850s with high hopes for a bright future on the burgeoning Iowa frontier.

From the beginning of their marriage troubles haunted the Sundays. No sooner had they started life together than the depression of 1857 set in, bringing a year and a half of panic with depressed wages, bank failures, and a decline in farm prices. Unable to get a farm of their own, William and Mary Jane Sunday built an unbarked log cabin on Mr. Corey's land, complete with two rooms, plank floors, and a flagstone chimney.

Children came quicker than economic success. A son, Albert, was born in 1858, and two years later Edward followed. By 1862 William Sunday was still farming some of his father-in-law's land, earning what he could on the side in construction, and looking forward to the day when he could buy his own farm.

The Civil War interrupted and then devastated the Sunday family plans. By February 1862 Mary Jane Sunday was pregnant with their third child. Nevertheless, after William got crops in he responded to the call for more volunteers. On August 22 he joined Company E of Iowa's Twenty-Third Volunteer Infantry Regiment. Eager to join Iowans who had already made news in battles at Pea Ridge, Arkansas, and Shiloh, Tennessee, he marched away as soon as the corn had been harvested.

The only family photograph of William Sunday shows him in a private's uniform, complete with brass buttons and flat-topped, leather-billed cap. A man with sensitive eyes, handsome nose and mouth, and heavy long beard, he posed for the picture in Iowa just before his regiment marched south into Missouri.

In the autumn of 1862 William wrote to his wife and asked her to name the baby William Ashley if it was a boy (no one knew who Ashley was for). It was his last letter home. A boy arrived on November 19. Five weeks later—three days before Christmas—Private William Sunday died of pneumonia. After drawing his last breath in a cold, damp army tent, he was buried in an unmarked grave in the wilds of Missouri.

Mrs. Sunday had a photograph and three children to remind her of William and a continual strain of hard circumstances to remind her that nothing much had gone well for any of them in the land of opportunity. Residing in a two-room cabin on a slice of her parents' land, she was not only husbandless, landless, and penniless, but she was burdened with a concern for her baby Willie, who had been ill from birth. For three years he was too weak to sit up or walk. Responding to the obligations of motherly devotion and familial responsibility, Mary Jane carried her youngest around with her on a crudely rigged tote pillow while she helped her parents plant corn, milk cows, chop wood, and wrangle horses.

The first stroke of good fortune after her husband's death came because of her generous nature. When a traveling doctor came through the area, she fed him and his horse and made him a bed in the garret. In exchange for his lodging and board, the country physician examined the frail child and then prepared a syrup made from local roots, leaves, and berries. For several weeks the hopeful widow faithfully fed her three-year-old the

7

potion. To the surprise of everyone but Mary Jane Sunday, young Willie gradually took on a robust color, gained strength in his limbs, and soon was normally growing and active.

For a season Mrs. Sunday continued to enjoy better times. Not only was her young child well, but she married again. Two children—a boy and a girl—blessed the union. Then tragedy struck once more. When the little girl was only three, she died from burns suffered in a bonfire accident. And not long after that her husband died too.

This surfeit of untimely death left an indelible mark on young Billy Sunday. He was only five weeks old when his father died, yet that loss stayed with him for the rest of his life. Three years before he died he published a little autobiography in installments for *The Ladies' Home Journal*. It begins with the words "I never saw my father." In the first few pages of this revealing memoir he recalls ten deaths in addition to that of his father. Four aunts and an uncle died of tuberculosis, and then a grandmother he dearly loved succumbed to the same disease. Billy was six years old when she died. "I would leave her coffin," he recalled, "only when forced to do so. The second day after the funeral my mother missed me. They called and searched everywhere; finally my dog picked up the scent and they followed my tracks through the snow to the grave, weeping and chilled through with the cold November winds. For weeks they feared I would not live."

Although he nearly died from lying on his grandmother's grave, Billy never gave up trying to remain linked in some way with those who died. His mother recalled that she had a small photograph of his deceased half sister, Libby, and the poor lad spent all of his hard-earned money to have an enlargement made which he kept all his life. In a similar quest many years later he made a search for his father's grave, giving up only after he was told that the remains had been exhumed and placed in an unmarked grave at Jefferson Barracks in St. Louis, Missouri.

As painful as these deaths all were, Billy Sunday soon experienced a more hurtful separation. By 1872 Mrs. Sunday and her parents were so impoverished that they could not feed and clothe all the children. The stricken widow was forced to make what had to be one of the most difficult decisions of her life—turning over the care of her sons to strangers. Her oldest son, Albert, who was nearly fifteen, was out on his own. But this left Ed (age twelve), Billy (age ten), and little Roy, a baby half brother. Roy did not qualify for the available state support because his father had not died in the war. Ed and Billy did qualify, however, and she felt she had no alternative to sending them away to the Soldiers' Orphans Home.

The parting in 1872 was so traumatic that Billy Sunday carried the scars throughout his life. He mentioned it in many sermons and recalled it in vivid detail in his autobiography. Much of the insecurity that he so clearly felt—particularly in personal and family relationships—certainly goes back to this time. His letters show a constant fear that he would be separated from those most dear to him.

Being sent to an orphanage in the nineteenth century was often very destructive. In some institutions the children were no better off than slaves. Happily, the Sunday brothers fared quite well. Thanks to the good offices of a state senator, they were assigned to one of Iowa's three well-run Civil War Soldiers' Homes located in Glenwood, about a hundred and fifty miles from the Sunday homestead. Billy remembered the departure this way:

> When we climbed into the wagon to go to town I called out, "Good-by trees, good-by spring." I put my arms around my dog named Watch and kissed him.
> The train left about one o'clock in the morning. We went to the little hotel near the depot to wait. . . .
> The proprietor awakened us about twelve-thirty, saying, "The train is coming." I looked into mother's face. Her eyes were red and her cheeks wet from weeping, her hair disheveled. While Ed and I slept she had prayed and wept. We went to the depot, and as the train pulled in she drew us to her heart, sobbing as if her heart would break.

9

The train reached Council Bluffs by sunrise, leaving the boys with several hours to wait for a train that would take .hem south to Glenwood. They had no money and nowhere to go. Billy recalled that they were "tired, sleepy, cold, hungry, and homesick." They wandered the streets of the Missouri River city and eventually found a hotel. Reluctant to walk in the main entrance, they went to the back door and asked for food. The wary cook initially suspected that they were runaways, but she changed her mind when they produced a letter of introduction to the orphanage. Exclaiming that her husband was killed in the war too, she took the boys into the kitchen where she filled them with buckwheat cakes and sage-flavored sausage. After letting the boys sleep by the fireplace all morning, the kindly woman awakened them for lunch before sending them on their way to the train.

This unnamed benefactor became a saint to Billy Sunday. He told the story of her generosity throughout his adult life. And in many sermons through the years he also honored the memory of the conductor who let the boys ride to Glenwood in his caboose despite their lack of funds. This railroad man, whose name is lost to history, not only provided the boys with a free ride but continued to stop off at Glenwood during the succeeding few months, climbing the hill to the Orphans Home and delighting the Sunday brothers with little gifts of candy, peanuts, and pennies.

Life at Glenwood became rather pleasant for Billy and Eddie. Despite their initial homesickness, they found the environment to their liking. The home was situated amid woods, fields, and rolling hills, the air was fresh, there were outdoor chores and activities, and Saturdays were given to walks, gathering wild food, or hunting squirrels and rabbits. Furthermore, although it is unlikely that the boys appreciated it, the quality of education there was superior to what they received at their one-room school in Story County.

But good things never seemed to last for the Sundays. No sooner had the boys settled in and begun to feel part of the landscape than the pain of separation reinfected their lives.

Eighteen months after they reached Glenwood, the state of Iowa decided to close two of the three Soldiers' Orphans Homes as an economy measure. Glenwood and Cedar Falls were shut, and all of the children were moved to Davenport, on the eastern edge of the state.

The three-hundred-mile trek to Davenport was not easy for the boys. Once again they said good-bye to familiar landmarks, and they were forced to bid a final farewell to the generous conductor. All of the orphans made the journey together, but they were forced to leave behind pets that they had come to love. Many of the children had their own dogs at Glenwood, and the youngsters in one voice begged to take them along. The administrators, however, had other plans. Billy reminisced in grievous detail about how their dogs were taken into the woods and shot despite the impassioned pleas of the children.

Billy Sunday seemed to see as much death as a small town undertaker, but he did not experience it without scars. He later recalled that from that day on he and his brother did all they could to avoid the man who killed their dogs, even though he moved with them.

Although the Davenport orphanage was similar to Glenwood in some respects—it was located in the country a short distance from town and had fields in which the children were required to do some farm labor—it had a markedly different physical plant. Glenwood had a single institutional building, but Davenport housed its significantly larger number of children (at least seven hundred, half boys and half girls) in thirty little cottages. The home placed approximately twenty-five orphans in each cottage and assigned a woman manager to each group.

The Davenport experience began in grief, but the boys adjusted well to their new surroundings. Indeed, Ed felt so good about his stay that several years after leaving he returned, serving the institution as carpenter and watchman. Billy never returned, but he took with him many fond memories and some important patterns for living.

It was Mr. and Mrs. S. W. Pierce, the superintendent and his wife, who made the orphanage a success. Mr. Pierce was a strict disciplinarian. He taught Billy to organize his days, do things on time, keep his uniform neat, and have a perpetual shine on his shoes. Mr. Pierce also assigned each boy a job. "What I learned there," said Billy, "opened the door in after years that had brought me where I am—I was taught to do my best. Do your best, that's all an angel can do. No one does his or her duty unless he does his best. More people fail from lack of purpose than from lack of opportunity."

At Davenport, boys who failed to shine their shoes or do their chores were denied passes on Saturdays. This was bad enough, but there was a worse fate for youngsters who tried to run away. Superintendent Pierce would always find the boys and bring them back. Then he would put them on a cinder driveway that encircled an oval park on the orphanage grounds. There they would march from eight in the morning until sunset every day for a week. Their only breaks were for lunch, dinner, and sleep.

If "hitting the cinders," as this punishment was called, gave young Sunday a look at punishment for transgression, Mrs. Pierce gave him an equally striking look at the gospel of forgiveness and love. A deeply devout woman who taught the children to pray and memorize Bible verses, Mrs. Pierce would talk to errant boys, "take them on her lap, and tell them how sad their mothers would be if they knew it." According to Billy "she would pray with them, and no one ever came from an interview with Mrs. Pierce dry-eyed."

The lessons learned from the Pierces ended in 1876, when Ed turned sixteen. Boys of that age were required to move on and make their own way in the world, leaving a bunk open to another homeless child. Billy could have stayed until 1878, but he chose to follow his brother rather than sever all ties with family.

The four years in orphans' homes were formative ones for Billy Sunday. They turned out to be some of the best years of his formal schooling. He left Davenport with an ability to read, write, and do elementary math. His legacy from the Pierces' care also included an ability to work hard and a desire to keep himself and his clothing neat and clean. Living in the Soldiers' Home taught him to get along with many people, and in the midst of hundreds of other youngsters he was freed from a temptation common to all children—the temptation to believe that he is the most important person in the universe.

The orphanage years also taught Billy Sunday some self-confidence. He not only discovered that he could perform all sorts of tasks; he also learned that among several hundred boys he was a first-rate athlete. More than once he was drawn into a fist fight, the most memorable being an unauthorized midnight rendezvous where he used his fists to lay out the school bully in the presence of scores of awestruck onlookers. During these years he also found that he was exceptionally fleet of foot. In a track meet he could beat anyone his age or older to the finish line. And on the baseball field he learned that his legs could do more than quickly get him under fly balls—they enabled him to steal bases.

By the time he left Davenport, fourteen-year-old Billy Sunday was beginning to feel good about himself. Able to read and write better than most rural Iowans, he could do anything from farm work to odd jobs, and he could take care of himself in a scrape. This budding self-esteem led him into a life of independence by the time he was fifteen.

After the Sunday brothers said their good-byes to the Pierces, Billy remembered that "we both left and went on the farm." Soon thereafter Ed hired himself out as a farmhand and handyman to a family with no sons, and Billy did farm work and chores for his grandfather and a Story County neighbor. This arrangement ended in a few months, however. One day Billy and his half brother Roy were helping their grandfather hitch up the horses. The old man was in a hurry to go to town when the boys began a tug-of-war on the neck yoke. "We pulled the rings out of the end," said Billy. "Grandfather was furious at our foolishness as it delayed him. He swore at us and it cut me to the heart. I'm of a sensitive nature."

Billy walked away from his grandfather's farm that day, vowing he would never return. From then on he proved to his family and himself that he could make it in the world alone. True to part of his vow, Billy supported himself from that day forward. He paid his way and lived on his own for the rest of his life, but there was no way he could ignore the family. He moved eight miles away to the city of Nevada, the county seat, where he secured a hotel job as a janitor, stable boy, porter, and clerk. Once during a bout with homesickness he begged for a night off. The leave was granted, and Billy walked out to see his family. When he returned twenty-four hours later than agreed, he found that he had lost his job and had no place to stay.

This reversal of fortunes was only temporary. Within a few days he secured a position doing chores in the home of a Civil War veteran and his wife. Colonel and Mrs. John Scott took Billy in, worked him hard, and gave him room, board, love, and attention. The Scotts also encouraged him toward self-improvement and helped make it possible for the young wanderer to stay with them and enter the Nevada high school. There is no evidence that Billy Sunday ever received a diploma, but he did stay in school for two more years, studying history, speech, geography, government, and literature. And regardless of whether he actually graduated, by 1880 he was much better educated than the typical American.

His education level notwithstanding, Billy Sunday was not well received in Nevada. Although it was a town of only several hundred people, it was a county seat with urban aspirations. To the high-toned townspeople, Billy Sunday was a bumpkin, and he chafed when people called him a "country jake." The only way he gained respect was through sports. One of his fondest memories was beating a professor from Ames in a hundred yard dash. The speedster also won respect when he played baseball for the Nevada team, but summer work as a field hand caused him to miss games and thereby forfeit his few chances for fun and respect.

In 1880, two months before his eighteenth birthday, Billy Sunday decided to give up the rural life. He said good-bye to the Scotts, further schooling, and the fields of Story County. He moved thirty miles east to Marshalltown, an agricultural service community that was becoming a small city. Sunday believed that Marshalltown could offer him a way out of the drudgery and stigma of farm labor, and the town had a baseball team with an impressive reputation.

The ambitious young man picked Marshalltown over Iowa's other communities with similar attractions because the Marshalltown Fire Brigade recruited him. In the late nineteenth century, volunteer fire departments competed to see who could get to blazes first. These contests evolved into regular tournaments where local and regional champion fire departments were judged on their ability to outperform the fleetest of foot from all over the state. The Marshalltown firemen had learned of Sunday's reputation for quickness and asked him to join them. His athletic prowess became his ticket from the farm, the key to the breaks he needed to alter his life.

Within two and a half years Sunday had made good on his determination to place himself beyond the need to return to farm labor. When he arrived in Marshalltown he not only joined the fire brigade but also secured a job with a local furniture store. A combination furniture-making and undertaking establishment, the firm hired the farm lad to help assemble and varnish everything from tables to coffins and to wrangle the horses and drive the hearse whenever they had a funeral.

While working in the furniture and undertaking business was not the love of Billy Sunday's life, it did afford him the leisure to play baseball each time the Marshalltown team took the field. The country jake from Story County not only made the team but immediately distinguished himself as a base stealer and left fielder. Playing regularly in the 1881 and 1882 seasons, he helped the team build a reputation as one of the best in the state. Indeed, by the end of the 1882 season Marshalltown had defeated every team they played in eastern Iowa, and the word spread across the counties that this team was Iowa's finest.

When the fame of Marshalltown reached Des Moines, the boosters of that city challenged the men from Marshalltown to come and play their undefeated team. The Des Moines crowd offered a side bet of $500 and gate money as well.

Late in the summer an eager team of Marshalltowners, escorted by an entourage of cheering local boosters, journeyed the ninety miles to Des Moines. By the end of the afternoon these small-town athletes had put their big-city rivals to shame. Billy had this recollection of his role in the victory: "We won the game 15 to 6. I played left field. Des Moines had some heavy right-handed sluggers, and our captain figured that I could get the fly balls. I had eight put-outs and made six of our fifteen runs."

That afternoon was one of Sunday's most memorable. Not only had he helped his teammates bring glory to Marshalltown, but he had also turned in a performance that would change his life. Unbeknownst to young Sunday, the Des Moines game was a watershed in his life. His effort that day broke, for a few years at least, a twenty-year succession of hard times.

2 Onward and Upward

1883-1891

"Boys, I bid the old life good-by."

It was in early spring 1883 that Billy Sunday received a telegraph message from Adrian Anson, captain and manager of the Chicago White Stockings. "That was the first telegram I had ever received," Sunday wrote in his autobiography, "and it was good news!" The good news was that "Pop" or "Cap," as the players called Anson, wanted Sunday in Chicago immediately to try out for the famous National League baseball team.

Cap Anson wintered in Marshalltown, Iowa, every year. The well-to-do Anson family resided there. Cap's father, Henry Anson, had donated to the county commissioners an entire block in the heart of the little city to be used for the site of the county courthouse. During Cap's sojourn in Iowa in the winter of 1882-83, his hibernation from baseball was interrupted regularly by his Aunt Em's graphic accounts of the exploits of Marshalltown baseball. Aunt Em, it seems, was one of the team's greatest fans. And she was no ordinary talent scout. Having traveled with the team for its state championship game with Des Moines, the enthusiastic lady was especially impressed by the performance of Billy Sunday. During Cap's off-season respite he heard many of her first-hand accounts of Sunday's athletic prowess, especially his speed.

Aunt Em had urged Cap to invite Billy to a White Stockings tryout, but the cautious professional made no promises. Nevertheless, once he assembled his team in 1883, assessed the talent, and examined their prospects, he decided to wire Sunday and give him a once-over.

In a remarkable display of self-confidence, the twenty-year-old bush leaguer resigned his job of finishing furniture, making mattresses, and driving the hearse. He spent his entire savings—$6.00—on a new sage-green suit. Then he borrowed $4.50 from a friend and spent $3.50 on the train trip to Chicago, so that he arrived with only one dollar in his pocket.

Although Chicago was only 250 miles from Marshalltown, as far as Billy Sunday was concerned the burgeoning midwestern metropolis might as well have been on another planet. The former farm boy had never been so far from Iowa, and he had never seen a city larger than Des Moines. When he arrived in Chicago the population was already well over a half million and growing fast. What Sunday saw as he approached the second largest city in America was a skyline of high-rise buildings, some of them seven, eight, even nine stories tall—taller than anything the Iowan had ever seen. And everything was shrouded by a thick cloud of black smoke produced by the coal and wood that heated and powered the city.

Chicago was a phenomenal metropolis at this time. Attracting worldwide attention as the nation's leading railroad center, the city boasted a business district that was advancing skyward as well as outward. The commercial center buildings were particularly remarkable because they were all brick, stone, or concrete—the consequence of a city ordinance passed in the wake of the great Chicago fire of 1871.

In addition to being impressed by the size and shape of individual buildings, Sunday must also have been impressed by their sheer number. He saw factories and warehouses in greater

18

numbers than he imagined existed in all of America. And while unpaved streets littered with horse droppings were nothing new to him, he had never seen anything like Chicago's collection of horse-drawn carriages, buses, and railcars.

He also witnessed the hustle and bustle of a motley population. The population of Chicago stood somewhere between one half and three quarters of a million souls, and over seventy percent of them were foreign-born or the children of foreign-born parents. The city was already teeming with newcomers from southern and eastern Europe, especially Italy and Poland, and he saw jostling among these people immigrants who had arrived earlier from northern and western Europe, in particular Germany, Ireland, and Scandinavia. To be sure, he had seen immigrants in Iowa, and he was not unused to hearing foreign languages spoken, but the vast numbers of foreigners in Chicago—indeed the sheer mass of people—daunted the newcomer.

Within an hour of arrival the small-town Iowan felt the anxiety and self-consciousness of a country bumpkin in the big city. He arrived at A. G. Spalding's Sporting Goods Store (Spalding was owner of the team) at 108 Madison, just as the telegram directed. But to his amazement no one was there at 7:00 A.M. "I wondered why the store was not open, as I had always gone to work when the whistle blew at seven o'clock." He recalled that he "sat on the curb until eight o'clock, when the store opened." Then he cooled his heels there for two more hours until the team members began to straggle in. The first man he met was A. F. Dalrymple, the left fielder of the Chicago club and champion batter of the National League. Gradually a few others came. "I was introduced to them," he agonizingly recalled. "My hair was long, and I sure looked like the hayseed that I was, compared to those well-groomed men, members of that famous old team."

After a while Cap Anson strolled in. Tall, rugged, and burly, he introduced himself to the uncomfortable newcomer. "Billy, they tell me that you can run some. Fred Pfeffer is our crack runner. How about putting on a little race this morning?"

19

Sunday happily agreed. Anything, he thought, to get out of his street clothes and on with his tryout. The tension eased somewhat as the team sauntered from Spalding's store to the ballpark on the lake front. The greenhorn borrowed a uniform from a pitcher named Larry Cochrane, but for the time being there were no athletic shoes. "Pfeffer came out and he had on running shoes, so I ran him barefooted, and I'm glad to be able to say that I ran rings around him, beating him by fifteen feet."

It was Sunday's speed that ultimately won him a permanent spot with the Chicago club, because this ingredient was part of Pop Anson's recipe for success. Anson was an enormous man for those days. He was six feet two inches tall, weighed well over two hundred pounds, and sported cleated baseball shoes that were a foot long. In 1880, at age twenty-eight, the big Iowa athlete took over Spalding's team as player-manager. From the outset Anson was an overwhelming success. Indeed, he was so popular, innovative, and effective that he left a permanent mark on professional baseball during the years 1880-1892, causing one historian to dub this era "The Age of 'Pop' Anson."

Anson led the White Stockings to five pennants during those years, and when they failed to take home the championship they always had the winners looking over their shoulders. They never finished lower than fourth place, and more often than not they were number two or three if they did not take the crown. Anson's successful strategy helped change the style of play all over the league. He pioneered the use of offensive and defensive signals, and he led the way in rotating pitchers. Anson also decided to build his teams with two kinds of athletes— heavy hitters and base runners with lightning-like speed.

Anson came along at a time when professional baseball was just reaching full blossom as the national pastime. The game began in the urban centers along the Atlantic coast in the 1850s, spreading westward as each new town tried to imitate the established towns in the east. Although baseball was played throughout America, in the growing urban centers it attracted large crowds and provided entertainment for factory and shop workers who needed an open-air outlet to escape the boredom and confinement of their jobs. By the 1860s urban political machines, especially in the big cities, gave organized baseball a big boost. New York's Tammany Hall, for instance, sponsored scores of amateur and professional teams, including the New York Giants. City politicians promoted the construction of large city parks, especially the kind used for big spectator events. They also urged the abolition of Sunday closing laws that prohibited games on the Sabbath. It was typical for political leaders to be in concert with urban transit owners, who stood to profit handsomely from the traffic that baseball created by attracting weekend recreation seekers.

As cities built more seating capacity into their ballparks so that hundreds and even thousands of onlookers could be accommodated, a few men like Chicago's Pop Anson helped make the game exciting. With power hitters who thrilled the crowds with extra-base drives and home runs, and daring base runners who taunted pitchers and infielders, Anson built an exciting team that, win or lose, always put on a good show.

The general prosperity of the 1880s, the nurture of politicians and transit magnates, and the growing effectiveness of managers' tactics and strategies conspired to promote baseball at this time. A strong economy made fifty cent admission affordable, and large attendance enabled owners to pay players big salaries and dress them in attractive uniforms.

Anson made Sunday a member of his twelve-man squad in 1883. The rookie played very little that first season—he took the field in only fourteen games—but he also served the team by handling all of the business management for Anson while they were on the road. Sunday collected Chicago's percentage of the gate, planned the travel schedule, and made hotel and train reservations. He always looked back with pride to the fact that the manager trusted him to carry the money and handle the accounts. The only story he repeated more often from his baseball days was about Anson having asked him that first day of tryouts how he was fixed for money. When Billy answered "I have one dollar," Pop handed him a twenty dollar gold piece. As Sunday put it in his autobiography, "that act would have endeared me for life had he done nothing else to help me, but he was always kind and good to me."

The player-coach had some good memories of Billy Sunday too, which he included in a book of reminiscences:

> The first thirteen times that Sunday went to bat after he began playing with the Chicagos, he struck out, but I was convinced that he would yet make a ball player, and hung on to him, cheering him up as best I could whenever he became discouraged. As a base runner his judgment was at times faulty, and he was altogether too daring, taking extraordinary chances because of the tremendous turn of speed he possessed. He was a good fielder, and a strong and accurate thrower, his weak point lying in his batting. . . .
>
> Sunday was, in my opinion, the strongest man in the profession on his feet, and could run the bases like a frightened deer. His greatest lack as a ball player was his inability to bat as well as some of the hard-hitting outfielders. He was a fast and brilliant fielder, a fine thrower, and once on first he could steal more bases than any of his team mates.

There were no minor leagues in the 1880s, no farm clubs where young players were seasoned and trained. Scouts simply visited hundreds of sandlots and schools in search of talent, and then brought the best prospects to the city for tryouts. As Sunday remembered, once you secured a chance to play you still had to prove yourself in the game. And "such aids as coaches for pitchers, catchers, infielders and outfielders, trainers, rubbers and doctors were unknown." As he put it, "you trained yourself. If the old heads on a team happened to take a fancy to you, they would offer suggestions; if not, you watched how they did the job and tried to imitate them."

One "old head" who helped Billy Sunday was Michael Kelly. Known as "King" Kelly by fans and teammates, he was a wild base runner and strong hitter. The seasoned veteran and first-stringer took the rookie aside after several strikeouts and helped him select a lighter bat. Billy said he taught him to "grasp my right hand at the end of the bat and my left hand about three or four inches farther up on my bat, and in that way I could hit quicker."

The results were not stellar, but the rookie showed marked improvement. Sunday batted .241 in fourteen games his first year, and he hit .222 after forty-three games in 1884. In 1885 he played in forty-six games, raising his batting average to .256. In 1886 Sunday played twenty-eight games and batted .243. During the season of 1887 he was a starter in fifty games and rapped out fifty-eight hits, pushing his average to a career high of .291. He also stole thirty-four bases that year.

The 1887 season was Sunday's last with the Chicago White Stockings. At the end of the year he was traded to another National League team, the Pittsburgh Pirates. The five years at Chicago, however, were pivotal in his life. First of all, he proved to himself that he could survive in the big city. Although not a first-stringer with the Chicagos, he was part of an elite squad of twelve. Furthermore he could now earn more money in a month than he could have made in a year in Iowa. He also learned that he could hit big-league pitching. And if hitting was not his strength, he at least got on base about twenty-five percent of the time he went to the plate. And when he got on base, he amplified his opportunities by stealing more bases than others on his team and most players in the National League.

Establishing himself as a professional ball player was important to the Iowa farm boy, but it paled in comparison to an event that took place during the 1886 season. The day and the month have been lost to history. In fact, Billy Sunday himself never remembered the precise date. It happened this way. One Sunday afternoon during the summer of 1886 Billy and some of the other players were walking the streets of Chicago. There were no games on Sundays in those days, and none of the half dozen players with Billy had anything purposeful to do. After a few drinks in a downtown saloon they strolled to the corner of Van Buren and State Streets. Parked on a vacant lot at the intersection stood a horse-drawn contraption called the Gospel Wagon. Sort of a rolling rescue mission complete with brass band, singers, and preacher, this mobile evangelistic program was in full gear on the Sabbath. "We sat on the curb listening to men and women playing on cornets and trombones and singing gospel hymns that many of the churches have blue-penciled as being too crude for these so-called enlightened days," wrote Sunday; "but these hymns stir memories that drive folks back to their mother's God and Christ."

What Billy Sunday encountered was a street-preaching team from the Pacific Garden Mission. Founded in 1877, less than a decade earlier, it was just one of several rescue missions that mushroomed in America's industrial cities after the Civil War. The urban industrial revolution of the post-war years brought jobs and upward mobility for many people, but the profound changes experienced in this period—especially during times of recession and depression—brought social and economic problems unprecedented in American life. Evidence of the magnitude of these problems could be found in the throngs of homeless drifters that wandered from city to city in search of food, clothing, and shelter. Some, of course, suffered from alcoholism and drug addiction, but many were simply down on their luck and out of work.

Beginning in New York City with such individuals as Phoebe Palmer and Jerry McAuley, evangelicals began to rent storefront buildings and offer outreach services. Coffee, rolls, and sometimes a hot meal were given to all who would come. Temporary lodging was provided, and second-hand clothing was distributed. Invariably an evangelistic religious service was held at least once a day, complete with music, Bible reading, prayer, and a sermon. From the beginning these urban missions were purposefully evangelistic. They offered relief to those without food, clothing, and shelter, but the primary focus was on ministry to the soul.

In keeping with this evangelistic focus, most city missions sent out horse-drawn "gospel wagons" to comb the streets where saloons, gambling dens, and houses of prostitution were most prevalent. A crowd would be attracted by the music, and soon a motley mob of onlookers—curiosity seekers, hecklers, and a few who were spiritually hungry—were in place and ready for an evangelistic message.

It was just such a street meeting that Billy Sunday was attracted to in 1886. It was the music that first drew his attention. The old Christian hymns stirred his memory and took him back to the family log cabin in Iowa. He could hear his mother singing gospel hymns while she cooked and sewed, and there was no doubt a tug at his heart for the old days at the orphanage in Davenport when Mrs. Pierce taught the boys Bible stories and encouraged them to pray. In the midst of his nostalgia a former counterfeiter and gambler named Henry Monroe stepped down from the gospel wagon, walked over to the men at the curb, and invited them down to Pacific Garden Mission to hear a message and learn about some people "who used to be dips (pickpockets), yeggs (safe-blowers), burglars, second-story workers, drunkards, and have done time in the big house, and who today are sober, honest, have good homes, and are trusted and respected." He urged them to come down to the mission and hear testimonies "of women who used to sell their womanhood to whoever would buy, were slaves to dope and drink, and are now married and have children of their own." Monroe encouraged the players to "come down to the mission and hear stories of redeemed lives that will stir you, no matter whether you have ever been inside of a church or have wandered away from God and decency."

Something inside Billy Sunday began to stir. Thirty years later he told his biographer that deep in his heart he felt dissatisfied. Despite his good salary and athletic success, there was an empty feeling. He longed for something more. Whatever the source of this inner restlessness, the veteran of three baseball seasons stood up at the street preacher's invitation and abruptly announced to his teammates on the curb, "Boys, I bid the old life good-by."

Billy remembered that "some laughed, some smiled, some shrugged their shoulders, and some looked with mingled expressions of admiration and disgust." In any case this clean-shaven and well-groomed young man got up on his powerful legs and followed that street evangelist and his entourage down to the Pacific Garden Mission. There Billy Sunday listened to more hymns and some testimonials about how a decision to follow Christ had brought changed lives. Then he heard a sermon encouraging the listeners to come to the altar, confess their sins, seek Christ's forgiveness, and set forth on a new pathway in obedience to Christ's teaching.

Billy Sunday listened to the preacher's invitation, but he did not go forward. Instead, he sorted thoughts and emotions and weighed the consequences. He instinctively knew that for him such a decision would have long-range implications. To be sure he felt somewhat unfulfilled, but he was uncertain about surrendering his personal agenda for life in order to receive a new one prescribed by Jesus of Nazareth.

That night Billy went away undecided, but there remained a turmoil in his soul. His schedule prevented a visit to the mission for several more days, but he went back later and attended meetings four or five evenings in succession. Like a window-shopper who never buys, he watched men and women walk forward to the altar rail and pray for Christ's forgiveness and for the Holy Spirit's direction for new life born out of a relationship with Christ.

Finally, after several nights of agony, the sun-bronzed ball player slowly went forward at the evangelist's invitation. Those legs that stepped into the batter's box with confidence and sped down the baselines with breath-taking speed and abandon were now unsteady—moving with the tentative deliberation of a frightened man unsure of his journey and destiny. It is tempting to see Sunday inching forward as a man on his way to the gallows, because that is precisely what the preacher called him to do. Billy remembered it was Harry Monroe who preached that night. He talked of death to one's self and death to the old life. He invited people to come forward to the altar, kneel down, and seek Christ's forgiveness for their old way of life. After praying, they would arise to a new life anointed by the Holy Spirit of God. They would walk out new people with a new start in life. Monroe knew what he was talking about from personal experience. He had heard this gospel just a few years before in the same hall, when the mission founder, Civil War veteran Col. George R. Clarke, called guilt-ridden sinners to the front. One night Monroe responded to the invitation, and he turned his back on a life of hard drinking, heavy gambling, and felonious crime.

A nervous Billy Sunday knocked over several curved-backed wooden chairs when he finally stood up to go forward. No doubt some people thought he was drunk—no small number of inebriates staggered their way to the altar rail when the evangelists called for sinners to come forward—but Sunday was not intoxicated. On the contrary, his mind was perfectly clear. His fumbling and hesitancy came from an inner sense that this trek to the front would indeed be the onset of a new life—a mere prelude to a wholly new pilgrimage.

It is true that plenty of people went forward at similar meetings and later evidenced little change in their lives. But Sunday's instincts suggested that for him this was no casual decision. Rather than a perfunctory gesture, this walk down the aisle for confession, repentance, and absolution would usher in changes as profound as those that came to Saul of Tarsus after he met the Spirit of Christ on the road to Damascus.

While twenty-three-year-old Billy Sunday struggled with his conscience and the chairs, Mrs. George R. Clarke—a former society woman known to the boys and men at the Mission as "Mother" Clarke—came and placed her arm around him. "Young man," she whispered, "God loves you. Jesus died for you, and he wants you to love him and give your heart to him." As Carl F. H. Henry put it in his history of the Pacific Garden Mission, "the ball player could no longer resist. He swung clumsily around the

27

chairs, walked to the front and sat down. Henry Monroe came to his side and they knelt for prayer." According to Billy's friend and biographer Elijah P. Brown, after Billy went forward, Mother Clarke pointed him to a cross on the wall. "Little by little she brought him to see clearly that eternal life is God's free gift, and being such, it must be received as a gift, through childlike faith in the finished work of Christ." Mrs. Clarke then gave Sunday some promises from the Bible, urged him to trust Jesus Christ for eternal salvation, and told him to obey God's commands.

According to Sunday's own testimony, several immediate changes came over his life as a result of this meeting. In retrospect, he saw it as the watershed event of his life. It was indeed a conversion or turnaround experience. The first manifestation of his new life was a relief from a sense of darkness and guilt that had haunted him—sometimes subtly, sometimes powerfully. It was, in his words, the removal of a great burden.

If this crucial event brought immediate relief, it also inaugurated a process that would not only change the ball player's life but would also affect the lives of hundreds, then thousands, and eventually hundreds of thousands of others as well. The first sign of this redirected life came within a few days after the conversion, when the Chicago ball club invaded St. Louis. No longer interested in drinking and gambling away his spare hours, the new believer found a secondhand book shop and invested thirty-five cents in a Bible. He had found a guidebook, and he wanted to ferret out those commands from God that Mother Clarke had urged him to obey.

Indeed, having purchased a Bible, Sunday proceeded to read it. Then on the next home stand he joined the Chicago Central YMCA Bible Training Class and embarked on a systematic study of the sixty-six books of Scripture. He also started attending the Jefferson Park Presbyterian Church on Chicago's fashionable West Side because it was handy to the neighborhood where most of the team rented rooms and it was within walking distance of the West Side Ball Grounds, where the White Stockings played when they were in town.

It became increasingly apparent to everyone who knew Billy Sunday that something fundamental had changed in his life. He stopped drinking alcoholic beverages of all kinds—including the cold beers ritually consumed after games by players and fans alike. To fill the free time that once was taken up at parties or in saloons, the Chicago outfielder started attending evening as well as the Sunday morning worship services. Because he was a household name among the ever-growing throng of baseball fans, the news of his conversion appeared in Chicago newspapers and in the dailies of every National League city in the country. Before long the word had spread to small cities and rural communities, as the editors of the smaller daily and weekly tabloids picked up the story.

Once it was known that Chicago's fleet-of-foot, base-stealing center fielder had become a Christian, numerous church and evangelistic organizations sought him out to give public testimony about his changed life. Among the scores of churches and agencies that asked Sunday to speak, no organization courted him more determinedly than the Young Men's Christian Association. Founded in London in 1844, it spread throughout North America during the next few years. By the late 1860s, Chicago had one of the largest and most vital YMCA programs. Under the presidency of Dwight L. Moody, the Chicago "Y" built a multipurpose building and established a series of programs designed to provide young city men with Christian alternatives to the evils of urban life.

From the 1850s until after World War I, North American YMCA programs were decidedly evangelistic. Reaching out first to young men but eventually to women and men of all ages, it set itself the goal of rescuing those who were perishing in a sea of urban problems. It called people to follow Christ and thereby find salvation from hell for their souls. It also called people to lead lives of temperance, good morals, hard work, and service so that they could bring glory to the God they promised to serve. That is to say, the YMCA set out first to make converts, and second to reclaim these converts into a new life of pure

morals and honest work. For many of the people they reached
this entailed getting them into Bible studies and Sunday schools
to be sure, but it also entailed feeding them, offering them
temporary shelter, and providing them with assistance in locat-
ing permanent employment and a place to live.

Officials of this unabashedly evangelistic YMCA sought
Billy Sunday to do some speaking for them. Within a few
months after his celebrated conversion, and after an initial rally
in Illinois, Billy was pressed to work in several cities speaking
to groups of anywhere from half a dozen to five hundred
teenage boys and young men. The Chicago press reported his
first public appearance this way:

> Center fielder Billy Sunday made a three-base hit at Far-
> well Hall last night. There is no other way to express the
> success of his first appearance as an evangelist in Chicago.
> His audience was made up of about five hundred men,
> who didn't know much about his talents as a preacher, but
> could remember his galloping to second base with his cap
> in hand.
>
> His talk was the most successful given in Farwell Hall
> for a year. He aimed straight at the young men in front of
> him, giving the truth in plain earnest language, and when
> he finished forty-eight of them raised their hands as
> seekers. After the regular service an inquiry meeting was
> held, in which Sunday took an active part, praying for and
> talking with the inquirers.

In New York City he was again asked to address a large
group of young men at the YMCA, and a local newspaper
reported the following:

> If W. A. Sunday plays ball as well and as earnestly as he
> talked yesterday before a large body of young men in the
> hall of the Young Men's Christian Association, he ought
> to be in great demand among the revival clubs. Although
> athletic young men were especially invited to hear the ball
> player, not many were present who were known to be

devoted to either professional or amateur athletics, but for all that the audience was a large one.

The reporter noted that the National League player urged the men to be serious about their faith. "God has no use for a milk-and-water man. To succeed in business, in a profession or in athletics, you have got to be in earnest," he told the audience. Within a few months Billy Sunday was teaching a Sunday school class at Jefferson Park Presbyterian Church, and he began offering regular programs at the Chicago YMCA. His popularity spread so rapidly that he could scarcely keep up with the calls to speak. The initial opportunities came because he was a sports celebrity, but the calls increased because he was an effective, captivating speaker. His natural way of talking and his knack for providing vivid illustrations attracted and held the listeners' attention. Some observers said he had a magical hold over his audience, and some of the devout said he was anointed and empowered by the Holy Spirit like Peter after Pentecost. But whatever the rhetoric used to describe his effect, it was agreed that he held audiences spellbound with his strikingly original, personal, and understandable applications of biblical texts. One early-day observer of Sunday's style said that "There was a charm and freshness about [his speaking] that was a constant surprise."

Evidently praying came as naturally. "He loved to pray," said a friend who knew him well in those early days. "Prayer was to him the natural expression of the worship that welled up in his soul, and it is not surprising that he was soon praying in public. He prayed because his heart was full of praise that could not be suppressed." Sunday's companion continued in this vein, noting that "whenever there was an opportunity to pray in the devotional meetings, others might hold back, but the young convert could not; and when he prayed all who heard knew that it was real prayer that he offered." His prayers were very natural, it was noted, and there was an urgency and expectancy about them as well. "He not only thanked God for what had been given, but put out his hands for more, in a way that left no doubt that he expected them to be filled."

At first the seasoned faithful in most communities were watchful if not skeptical. In their years of Christian service they had seen their share of enthusiasts make a big noise in the first blush of conversion and then fade out once the newness wore off. But with Sunday there was something different. He not only kept going forward, he sought out older saints who had been on the pilgrim trail much longer than he and learned from their companionship and guidance.

There was another difference too. Wherever he went, people wanted to hear him speak, but he did not seek the limelight on his own. Furthermore, wherever he spoke he told people about the problem of sin, and that it was only Jesus Christ who could relieve their bondage and guilt. It was also true that whenever he delivered his blunt if colorful talks, people responded. When he asked for a decision to confess sins, repent, and start a new life with Christ, folks always raised their hands or walked forward to the altar. In short, from a quantifiable perspective, his speaking was markedly effective.

As the 1886 baseball season ended, another change came into Billy Sunday's life. One evening a friend introduced him to Helen Amelia Thompson at a Jefferson Park Presbyterian Church social. She was an attractive eighteen-year-old who served as a member of the Christian Endeavor Society and as superintendent of the Sunday school's intermediate department. Helen, or Nell as her friends knew her, was the daughter of William Thompson, well known as the owner of the city's largest dairy products business. Nell was an attractive woman who stood about five feet four inches tall and had black hair and black eyes. She and her family lived across the street from the church at 62 Throop Street, and all members of the Thompson family were viewed as pillars of the church and society.

Sunday was smitten. He wrote in his autobiography that "the first time I saw those flashing black eyes and dark hair and white teeth, I said to myself, 'There's a swell girl.' . . . After several weeks I braced up one evening and asked Miss Thompson if I could see her home." She shied off for a minute, he recalled, but she "then smiled and said, 'Yes,' and from that time on I was hooked."

Nell Thompson obviously returned an interest in the ball player who was four years her senior, but she was dating another young man, and she was not as taken by Billy as he was by her. At first she viewed him as just another decent and eligible man, and she introduced him to one of her best friends who was at the time without a steady date. But Billy only had eyes for Nell. He broke off a long-distance relationship with a young woman in Iowa, and he went to prayer meetings and sat in a strategic place where he could, as he recalled, "keep one eye on Nell . . . and the other on the preacher." When her steady beau missed a church meeting one night, Billy moved in on Helen with his usual swiftness, imploring her to allow him to escort her the hundred yards from the church to her front door.

Nell agreed, and eventually Billy's persistence paid off. From then on he walked to the baseball park via Throop Street. He passed her house each day that the team was in Chicago. In fact, he made the trip past her house four times daily—walking from his hotel to the park for ten o'clock practice, home for lunch, back for practice or the 3:45 game (they almost always played at 3:45), and then once again in the evening. Eventually Billy noticed that Nell swept the front steps and sidewalk four times a day, just as he went by. And as it stayed light until after the games were well over, she increasingly ventured out at the time of his post-game jaunt and inquired about the score. He was especially encouraged when he noticed that "if we had an extra-long game, she swept on until I showed up. I would explain the game, who won or lost, how many hits and runs I made."

A persistent wooer from the outset, Billy finally persuaded Nell to break off the courtship with her other suitor. Nevertheless, the love-struck ball player soon discovered that winning her heart was only part of the battle for her hand. Mrs. Thompson liked Sunday because he was a dedicated Christian, albeit a recent convert. Mr. Thompson, on the other hand, was set against the relationship. He was a serious-minded businessman of Scottish ancestry who rejoiced in hard work and frugality. A Civil War veteran who was badly wounded in 1863 at the Battle of Shiloh, he made his way back from agonizing wounds and started a dairy products manufacturing business in the boom years after the war. A midlife convert himself, Mr. Thompson admired Sunday's commitment to Christian living, but he had no use for professional baseball. To his mind ball players were late adolescents—men who refused to work for a living and spent their time playing and drinking beer. Although National League players earned increasingly high salaries, Thompson saw them as transient ne'er-do-wells who were unstable and destined to be misfits once they were too old to play.

There was some truth to the senior Thompson's view. Professional ball players had well-earned reputations as hard-drinking and fast-living dandies, and not a few of them ended up on skid row after their playing days were over. That Billy Sunday was not drinking and that he spent his spare hours studying Scripture and spreading the gospel were not lost on Nell's father, but it was many months before he relented and allowed the Chicago White Stocking in his house. Until spring of 1887, Billy and Nell were restricted to seeing one another at church or on the occasions when Nell ventured down to the ball-park in the winter to ride on the commercial slide that Pop Anson owned and paid Billy to operate in the off-season.

Billy's new range of off-diamond activities—courting, public speaking, teaching, and Bible study—do not seem to have hurt his baseball career. Although the Chicago team dropped to third place in 1887 after a first-place finish the season before, it was Billy's best season yet. Playing in fifty games (almost twice as many as the previous year), he got fifty-eight hits, raising his batting average higher than ever before (to .291), and he stole thirty-four bases.

But if dating Helen Thompson improved Sunday's baseball performance, her influence was even greater in other ways. She was a more mature Christian than Billy, despite the fact that he was nearly four and a half years older than she. The result of this disparity, however, was not tension. On the contrary, she quietly and gently led him into pathways of spiritual maturity that gave him a more effective influence when speaking. And Helen did more than serve as one of Billy Sunday's spiritual directors; she began teaching him how to behave in polite company. She was, after all, much better educated than this recent refugee from rural Iowa, having graduated from an outstanding urban high school. Billy never received a high-school diploma, and the country schools he had attended were inferior to those of Chicago in any case. He had never been exposed to middle-class manners and customs. At the orphanage he had learned to keep his clothes clean and his shoes polished, but he had attained only a limited vocabulary, his grammar was not always correct, and he had not encountered a need for middle-class etiquette until he arrived in Chicago and attended a middle- to upper-income church.

It was probably Helen Thompson's influence that led Billy to enroll in classes during the winter of 1887-88 at the Evanston Academy, a college preparatory school located on the campus of Northwestern University. The university had been looking for a professional baseball player to coach their college team in the fundamentals of the game. When Billy got the job, he began taking classes on the side at the prep school. His personal letters from the 1880s show that his English grammar and usage skills were weak, and we can surmise that his public speaking needed polishing as well. In any case, he spent the winter in Evanston taking courses in English and rhetoric and coaching the university ball team.

Several letters between Billy and Nell written during that winter have survived. Taken as a whole, they provide insights into the character of each person and into the nature of their relationship. They show that the couple was already very much in love, although Nell's father was still unhappy about their

35

courtship. One letter reveals that they visited whenever Billy could find time to take the train to Chicago. Nell evidently made an excursion or two up to Evanston too. On one visit in Chicago, Billy managed to escape just moments before Nell's father came down the steps into the basement where they had been seeing one another. On another occasion Mr. Thompson found one of Billy's love letters to Nell, and he was displeased to say the least. The correspondence shows, too, that she encouraged him in his studies and supported him in the quest to polish his skills. Her letters sometimes contained an expression or phrase that she assumed he did not know. She would use the phrase and then tactfully explain its meaning in the text.

These letters show more than Helen's attempts to improve Billy's vocabulary; they give evidence of some psychological traits as well. It is not surprising, given Sunday's early life, that his correspondence manifests profound insecurities. Even after he proposed marriage on New Year's Day 1888 and she immediately accepted, he was fearful of losing her love. In early February 1888 she wrote to reassure him: "My darling Will," she began, "remember that Nell will always stay by you *no matter what may happen*. Can I put it plainer than that. My devotion for you is all my life's happiness so I intend to keep it." Two months later this devout twenty-year-old demonstrated how well she instinctively understood that her betrothed needed the love of a mother as well as a lover and wife. To the orphan who had experienced so many separations and losses she wrote, "my poor lonesome little baby. All he needs is his mama and he would be perfectly happy."

Their separation while Billy was at Evanston was difficult enough for him to bear, but his homesickness for Nell grew much worse during the 1888 baseball season. In an attempt to rebuild his team, A. G. Spalding made a number of changes, one of which involved his speedy outfielder: Billy was traded to the Pittsburgh Pirates. This meant that he would not be able to see Nell for extended periods throughout the summer—a prospect that was made somewhat less bleak when Mrs. Thompson finally won her husband over to the idea of Nell's marriage to a baseball player and a September 1888 wedding was planned. The promise of an autumn union went a long way toward helping the new Pittsburgh outfielder cope with the time and distances that kept him from his fiancée. His spirits were also buoyed by the fact that he was more important to the Pirates than he had been to the Stockings; he now played first string and was needed almost every game.

Billy Sunday played 120 of Pittsburgh's 134 games that season. He averaged a hit for nearly every game he played, getting a total of 119. Hired for his speed as much as for his hitting, the now-famous base runner stole 71 bases his first year with the Pirates, although he only batted .236.

The rewards of the season notwithstanding, Billy had a difficult time coping without Nell by his side. His letters to her during the summer of 1888 show that he was desperately lonely and despondent. He kept her picture in his Bible so that he would see it each time he opened the Scriptures. During the spring and summer that year he wrote to Nell daily. Telling her of his loneliness, he sought her approval for staying in his room when they were rained out rather than going on the saloon circuit with the other men.

Billy appears to have spent the evenings writing to Nell and feeling sorry for himself. He was only upbeat on Sunday and Wednesday nights after he had attended prayer meetings in a nearby church. Eventually Nell tired of Billy's attitude and assumed a role she would have to play throughout their nearly fifty years together. She put her foot down and let Billy know she had had enough of his self-pity. Get your mind back on the game, she told him, or it will wreck this season, ruin your chances for next year, and ultimately harm our marriage. "Everybody likes you and appreciates you. Now brace up and throw off that burden that pulls you down and be the strong, stout hearted man that you are." Her father had to be gone much of the time, she continued, and he never behaved that way. "Stop it right now," she exclaimed. "Your body will have to give way to your mind and brain fever will result." Then, only half apologetically, she said, "I had to write this. It can't go on." This strong rebuke was precisely what Sunday needed. After he had received it, his game improved and his letters grew positive. He understood her need to set him straight. "I feel well [and] not quite as lonesome as I did." She replied that it hurt to tell him off, but the result was important. In reply he sent a "cheerful and loving letter."

With Billy more stable and the season drawing to a close, Helen and Bill were married in Chicago in September. "I left the team in Indianapolis," Sunday wrote in his autobiography. "[We] were married on September 5, 1888, by Dr. David C. Marquis, of McCormick Theological Seminary, of Chicago, at two o'clock in the afternoon." Immediately after the ceremony the couple went to the ball grounds where Sunday's former boss, A. G. Spalding, had a box draped in decorations for them. The crowd gave the happy couple a standing ovation, and Sunday's old teammates lined up in front of the box, took off their hats, and wished the couple a lifetime of bliss. "We left Chicago for Pittsburgh on the Pennsylvania Limited at five o'clock," he wrote, and the next day in Pittsburgh he suited up and started in left field.

During the remainder of the 1888 season Mrs. Billy Sunday traveled with her husband and they maintained a flat in Pittsburgh. Neither of them liked their new home. A Pennsylvania steel manufacturing city with a population of 344,000, Pittsburgh was smaller than Chicago and much dirtier. They left the city once the season was over and made their way back to Chicago, the place they would always name as home. "Mother," or "Ma," as Billy endearingly referred to his bride, tended to housekeeping in their small flat, and he took Bible classes at the YMCA. He also did plenty of speaking and preaching as well as some volunteer evangelistic work for the YMCA.

The previous off-season Sunday had coached at Northwestern, and the season before that he worked as a fireman for the Chicago and Northwestern Railway. But during the winter of 1888-89 he stayed at home, devoting himself to study and ministry, and getting to know his wife.

One of the results of the stay-at-home winter was the strengthening of Billy's relationship with his father-in-law. Mr. Thompson grew to like his son-in-law, and he even gave them money to allow Nell to travel with him during the next baseball season. "I suppose the fact that he was an old soldier, member of the 51st Illinois . . . and that my own father was a member of the 23d Iowa, helped to establish a bond of sympathy," Sunday wrote later.

The 1889 season, though not Sunday's best, was certainly respectable. He played in 81 games, got 77 hits, and stole 47 bases. His batting average was .240, and he helped the Pirates climb from sixth to fifth place.

The following winter the family of one year returned to Chicago. Billy again worked without salary for the YMCA, and he studied Scripture with renewed intensity.

Early winter 1890 brought several changes to the Sunday home. In late January Mrs. Sunday gave birth to their first child, who was named Helen after her mother. The little girl's arrival meant that Mrs. Sunday could no longer take trips with her circuit-traveling husband.

About this time, Mr. L. W. Messer, the director of the YMCA, asked Billy if he would consider leaving baseball and working full-time for the "Y" as an evangelist, Bible instructor, and head of the department of religion. But Sunday did not see how he could adequately provide for his new family with the small salary the YMCA was offering, and so he turned down the offer. Still, the idea played powerfully on his mind. As the snow melted and the first signs of spring appeared, the baseball player began to feel the call of the diamond, but he also felt a longing in his soul for a different way of life.

Billy was twenty-seven years old when the 1890 season opened, and he was just reaching his stride as an athlete. After eighty-six games with Pittsburgh, his batting average was .257. The season was two-thirds finished when he was traded to

Philadelphia, where he played thirty-one more games and batted .261. He stole eighty-four bases during the entire season and gained enough fame as a base runner that he was interviewed on base stealing for a how-to manual published that year.

When the season ended, Billy Sunday was offered his best salary ever in the National League. The owner of the Philadelphia club asked him to sign a three-year contract at nearly $400 a month for the seven-month season. At that time the average industrial worker earned only about $380 per year. The money looked especially useful to the Sundays by the winter of 1890-91. Not only did they have a baby to care for, but Billy's brother Albert had become an invalid and needed financial support. And Billy's mother again fell on hard times. Not only was she unable to help Albert, but she stood in need of assistance herself.

These financial burdens notwithstanding, Billy Sunday spent the winter of 1890 wondering if he should be in full-time Christian work. His family needed help, to be sure. But if God wanted him to spend his life speaking to people who were hurting like he had been a few years earlier, then how could he continue to play ball?

As the hard freeze of the new year settled in on the Windy City, Billy felt increasingly certain that he was being called into ministry. He agonized over the three-year commitment he had made to Philadelphia the autumn before. In her little memoir Ma Sunday remembered his turmoil:

> He said, "I know . . . it is more money than Pittsburgh paid, and more money than Chicago paid; but, you know, I kind of feel the Lord is calling me to give my full time to Christian work." And he said, "Three years looks like a very long time to me now as I think about it. If you don't mind, I would like to send a request for my release."

Nell was not enthusiastic about the idea of a release. From the beginning of their relationship, money had been a problem. When she met Bill he was a spendthrift. Indeed, she had to teach him frugality much as she encouraged him to improve his English and stop his self-pity. He never gambled or drank after he was a believer, but he still knew nothing about managing his finances. This is not really surprising, since he had never had much money to worry about. Nell, on the other hand, came from a business-oriented family, and she had spent some time in business college between her high-school years and their marriage in 1888. In a sense, it fell to her to deal with their increased financial responsibilities. She urged caution before giving up a large salary. Perhaps it was a gift from God for the express purpose of allowing them to care for Albert, Billy's mother, and baby Helen. But despite her inner concerns, Nell was too devout to put mammon before God's call on their lives. Finally she told Billy that if this call was from God, then he should ask for a release. "The Lord isn't talking to me about it," she said, "but if he's talking to you, pay attention. . . ." The next day Billy went to the YMCA to study and pray before he sent a telegram to Philadelphia seeking a release. The following day the answer came and it was an emphatic No.

After reading the telegram, Billy relaxed. He believed that it was now God's responsibility to arrange a release before he had to report for training in late March. If such heavenly intervention was not forthcoming, Billy was prepared, as an honest man, to stand by his agreement for three more seasons. Although his heart was somewhat heavy, he determined to make the best of a situation he could not in good conscience change. He had tried to respond to the call and the way seemed to be incontrovertibly blocked.

But then, to the amazement of Nell and Billy, the Philadelphia management had a last minute change of heart. He later wrote, "on the 17th day of March, St. Patrick's Day—I shall never forget it—I was leading a meeting and received a letter from Colonel Rogers, president of the Philadelphia Club, stating I could have my release." As soon as Jim Hart of the Cincinnati team heard about it, he found Sunday at the YMCA and put a contract in his hands for $3,500—or $500 a month for a seven-month season. This was over a hundred dollars a month more than most workers earned in a year.

Sunday had, in his own words, "told God if he wanted me to quit playing ball to get my release before the 25th day of March and I would quit." But here was an even higher offer than he had with Philadelphia, and it required only a one-year commitment. When the March 17 telegram arrived he was confident of God's will and intervention, but now the Cincinnati offer complicated and confused everything.

Billy immediately went around to friends for advice. Some told him to grab Cincinnati's offer while others told him to stick to his promise. His father-in-law said, "You are a blank fool if you don't take it," but this time Nell did not agree. She felt they had made a covenant with the Lord and they should be faithful.

That night Sunday stood at a fork in the road. "I went to bed, but could not sleep, and prayed that night until five o'clock."

3 The Apprenticeship

1891-1896

"He does not look like a preacher."

Discerning God's will was not always easy for Billy Sunday, but after spending the night of March 17 in prayer, he believed the telegram was from God. The Cincinnati offer, he concluded, was a diabolical diversion. Sunday immediately accepted Mr. L. W. Messer's offer of $83.33 a month to work for the YMCA. When he hung up his baseball glove and shoes for good, his father-in-law shook his head in disbelief. How could his son-in-law exchange a promise of $3,500 for seven months' work for a six-day-a-week job at $1,000 annually with very little vacation?

If the decision made no sense to Mr. Thompson, it nonetheless brought peace of mind to Billy and Ma—at least most of the time. Billy knew that year-round evangelistic work was his calling, but when money was so short that there was barely enough to pay the rent, he sometimes wondered if he had accurately heard the Lord. Money grew tighter still in 1892, when their second child, George Marquis, was born. And an aging Mrs. Sunday and long-suffering Albert continued to depend on Billy for help.

The Sundays' financial burden eased somewhat the following year when Albert died and Billy's mother remarried for a third time. Billy's YMCA salary scarcely increased at all, but it did prove adequate to meet the needs of the smaller circle of dependents. The family managed to make ends meet, the new work was fulfilling, and they saw this as ample evidence that they were in God's will.

Indeed, the Sundays were grateful for their modest income when a nationwide depression during the winter of 1893-94 brought mass unemployment, tight money, a collapsed stock market, and widespread misery. Homeless men, women, and children roamed the streets of Chicago and other American cities seeking food, shelter, and work. They rode railway boxcars from one city to another looking for jobs. By the summer of 1894 even the rural areas of America were being invaded by these bedraggled exiles from the cities, who hoped to exchange field-hand work for a few pennies plus room and board.

Tramps were as common across America by 1893 as soldiers in uniform had been thirty years earlier. While poverty ravaged every corner of the nation, it struck hardest in the cities, where ailing industries were forced into massive layoffs. The Sundays could see that unemployment was no respecter of class, race, or religion, and like many Christians of the 1890s they had to make decisions about the focus of their ministry.

To what extent the Sundays were influenced by the outpouring of literature on the subject of Christian orthodoxy and its response to poverty we do not know. No evidence remains to show if either Billy or Nell read such hotly debated books of the time as Mrs. Humphrey Ward's *Robert Elsmere,* William Dean Howells's *A Traveler From Altruria,* William T. Stead's *If Christ Came to Chicago,* or Charles Sheldon's *In His Steps*—first serialized in a Chicago newspaper *(The Advocate)* and then published in book form. Whatever their reading habits, we do know that the Sundays were not out of touch with the times. They knew of the debates raging in the press, in seminaries, and consequently in the pulpits and Sunday school classes. All around them were discussions and arguments over the church's priorities. Should the church work to feed the poor and alter an economic system that was leaving so many helpless and hurting, or should it be concerned with telling all people—rich and poor—that they are sinners and that only Jesus Christ can forgive sins and provide a way back into a loving relationship with God?

Not all Christians saw these choices as mutually exclusive propositions by any means. But it is true that the strongest advocates of each alternative marked ends of an increasingly polarized spectrum in the church. The influence of modern scholarship and biblical criticism, growing largely out of the German universities, led many theologians to reevaluate the gospel message, to place less emphasis on the hereafter and more on the here-and-now. The new scholarship began with the premise that the Bible should be studied with the same body of tools and insights used to analyze other writings and phenomena. The more extreme advocates of this view eventually abandoned the idea that the Bible is any more divinely inspired than any other book, rejected reports of miracles in the Old and New Testaments, and adopted the doctrine of universalism—the belief that Christ died to save all of mankind and hence that no one will go to hell. Even among less radical liberals, there was generally less concern about an individual's eternal fate and more concern about the immediate misery of a growing body of economically displaced men and women. A growing number of Christian leaders, especially graduates of prestigious eastern seminaries, believed with deep conviction that the church was called to work to usher in the kingdom of God on earth. Their efforts to promote equality of opportunity for the oppressed, even to the extent of using the church as a tool for economic, political, and social change, were variously categorized as "Christian Socialism," the "Social Gospel," and the like. Christ came to set the captives free, they said, and the church must continue to pursue this divine objective.

Largely in reaction to the spread of the new liberalism, a

new conservative movement sprang up as well. Dedicated to a renewal of emphasis on what they defined as the fundamentals of the Christian faith, some members of the movement came in later years to be known as fundamentalists. They insisted that the Bible was the inspired, inerrant Word of God, and they placed special stress on those points of interpretation and doctrine where they differed with the liberals—on the literal accuracy of the miracles accounts, for instance, and on the virgin birth, the divinity of Christ, the reality of heaven and hell, and so on. Predictably, their evangelistic efforts were focused much more on attaining personal salvation than on solving social problems.

Then as now, most Christians and Christian groups stood somewhere between the liberal and conservative extremes. The Salvation Army, for example, worked both to feed, clothe, and rehabilitate the poor and also to spread the gospel story of Jesus' death and resurrection for sinners. Urban missions such as Chicago's Pacific Garden and Olive Branch also proclaimed the gospel while feeding and clothing the poor. Nevertheless, Salvationists and rescue mission workers saw their first priority as evangelism. To their mind the Bible made it clear that all men and women are separated from God because of their sinful natures and that all who die without God spend eternity in hell. The only remedy for this dreadful fate is the good news that Jesus Christ died for everyone's sins, and those who acknowledge this and call on his name for forgiveness will be saved from eternal damnation.

Billy and Nell Sunday were as much caught up in the swirl of social, religious, and economic ideas as other Christians. Unlike the thoughtless multitudes who could remain uncommitted—who could finally drift with the flow of consensus—temperamentally the Sundays had no choice but to think through the issues and take a position. As a family they were, after all, committed to full-time ministry. Furthermore they were people of strong opinions. Daily they heard the debates, because it was in the YMCAs, in Sunday school classes, and in the

Endeavor societies that these timely issues were raised. From their vantage point they could see that the tide, especially among fashionable people by the 1890s, seemed to be going with the liberals. It was becoming voguish to question the veracity of Scripture. And if not all of the better educated people wanted to reform or revamp the economic system, many of them found in the doctrine of universalism a convenient and respectable rationale for giving up the difficult work of evangelism.

As Billy Sunday had done before when he faced the question of staying in baseball or entering full-time ministry, he took this issue to prayer. He was not afraid of change. Indeed, he had moved about in his thirty years, and he had attempted more than one major shift in career. And he instinctively identified with the poor. He had experienced the burdens of poverty firsthand from the time of his birth until he entered major league baseball. The members of his family—including his mother and his aunt—were unable to escape their marginally impoverished existence until he was able to help them in the twilight of their lives.

Finally, however, Sunday's inclinations toward a ministry of social reform were counterbalanced by his own experience. He had found economic success in the early 1880s, and yet his life had lacked fulfillment and purpose. It was evangelists, not social reformers, who had pointed him toward Jesus Christ. And his relationship with his Lord and Savior was based on the Bible, in particular the four Gospels. Beyond this, Billy Sunday's original call—and he believed it was a divine call—was to go and point other sinners and lost people to the Savior he knew. He would be generous to the poor always, but as far as the focus of his ministry was concerned, the die was cast: he would do the work of an evangelist.

After getting his moorings through prayer, he began to take an even bolder stand for biblical Christianity in a most literal and fundamentalist sense. He preached and gave his testimony whenever opportunities occurred, and he spent his days and evenings finding speakers for noonday prayer meetings and evening classes. When his schedule allowed, he could be found doing the work of a home missionary. His friend and biographer Elijah P. Brown noted that during his three years with the YMCA he often spent days "visiting the sick and destitute, praying with the troubled, comforting the afflicted and burying the dead." Brown observed that "at one hour he might be going about among the saloons, distributing cards of invitation to meetings and urging those he found there to attend, while the next he might be on his knees praying for some despairing man who had just been making a fruitless attempt at suicide."

After Sunday's first year with the YMCA, the directors tried to persuade him to give up his work in the religion department and take over the program of physical culture and gymnastics. Because he was a good administrator as well as a natural athlete with a reputation in sports, they decided he was the man to handle the larger, growing physical education program. But as Brown recalled it, Billy Sunday did not want to give up "trying to raise money enough to save some poor mother with a brood of little children and a drunken husband from being set out on the street." Being restricted to the gymnasium would take him away from "contact with many people who needed all the help that God could give them." His daily evangelistic endeavors "quickened his own faith, for he had many opportunities of seeing that God 'is mighty to save, and strong to deliver.' "

Sunday's toil among the flotsam and jetsam of Chicago society convinced him more than anything else of sin's reality. He came to believe that no kind of reform program—political, economic, or social—could clean up the pollution in the city. He stated to Elijah Brown that "nothing short of absolute regeneration would ever stop and heal the awful ravages of sin. To attempt reform," he believed, "in the black depths of the great city would be as useless as trying to purify the ocean by pouring into it a few gallons of spring water." Consequently, from the beginning his teaching and his preaching were saturated with biblical references, and his constant refrain was that everyone had to "get right with God" through repentance and a personal relationship with Christ.

Billy Sunday's boldness to proclaim the biblical message of sin and salvation through Christ did not go unnoticed. In a time when increasing numbers of preachers were toning down their messages to avoid offending anyone, Sunday spoke with unusual candor and clarity. Whether one agreed with him or not, it was clear that he knew what he believed and was unequivocally enthusiastic about it.

Sunday's reputation as an evangelist grew during his time with the YMCA. After less than three years in the post, he received an opportunity that was eventually to launch his own independent evangelistic ministry—a ministry that he would pursue until his death in 1935.

It happened this way. The Rev. J. Wilbur Chapman, possibly the best-known evangelist in America by the 1890s except for the aging Dwight L. Moody, was in Chicago on numerous occasions during the mid-1890s. Born in 1859 in Richmond, Indiana, Chapman was just three and a half years older than Billy Sunday but light-years ahead of him in advantages and experience. Chapman was born into a well-to-do family. Although his mother died when he was thirteen and his father lost all of their money while J. Wilbur was a boy, the family eventually recouped their losses and set out on a prosperous course once again. By 1876 young Chapman was sent to Oberlin College at his father's expense. After one year in an academic environment still rich with memories of Charles Grandison Finney, Chapman transferred to Lake Forest College in Illinois. From there he ventured into Chicago to hear the famous Dwight L. Moody preach. Chapman claims that he could never remember not believing in Jesus Christ as his personal savior. Nevertheless at one of Moody's services in 1877 he went to the prayer room afterward to counsel with the famous evangelist and make certain of his salvation.

Chapman's life was changed that night. At age eighteen he was confident of his salvation and equally certain of his call to do the work of an evangelist. Indeed, by 1879 he was enrolled at Lane Seminary in Ohio, and from there he entered pastoral ministry in 1882.

Chapman stayed in touch with Moody from 1877 onward. He frequently visited the Moody Bible Institute and he shared in a number of summer conferences with Moody. When the elder evangelist was invited to more conferences than he could attend, he recommended Chapman to go in his stead. The world-famous evangelist was becoming Chapman's mentor, and he encouraged the young seminary graduate to preach evangelistically to the lost and make faithful, well-informed disciples out of timid believers. Subsequently Chapman pastored a church, preached revivals all over the Midwest, and conducted Bible conferences during the summers for believers.

In January 1884, Moody introduced Chapman to the Rev. Sol C. Dickey, a well-known preacher in the upper Midwest. He encouraged both of these men to launch a summer conference center at Winona Lake, Indiana, about a hundred and fifty miles east of Chicago. Thanks to their efforts, the center was opened the following summer with over 350 eager souls in attendance to hear conservative Bible teaching.

During the Chicago World's Columbia Exposition in 1893, Moody arranged an evangelistic outreach. He did not want to miss an opportunity to tell the gospel story to hundreds of thousands of visitors from all over the world. J. Wilbur Chapman was one of the evangelists he recruited to speak in Chicago during the Exposition.

It was probably during the winter meetings in 1893 that Chapman first learned about Billy Sunday. The previous year Chapman had left the pastoral ministry to devote full time to evangelistic preaching and summer Bible conferences. Not yet teamed up with his famous song leader, Charles M. Alexander, he had at this time a musician and singer named Peter Bilhorn. Billy Sunday and Bilhorn had become friends through the YMCA, and it was Bilhorn who introduced his Chicago friend to the increasingly famous evangelist.

When Billy Sunday met Chapman, the college-educated, seminary-trained preacher was almost thirty-five years old. An ordained Presbyterian, Chapman was suave and urbane. He dressed like a banker, no doubt learning good taste in clothes from his businessman father and his well-heeled classmates in college. He had round, gold-rimmed glasses, pursed lips, and a large dimple above his upper lip that accentuated his Roman nose; his hair was neatly combed and conservatively parted on the left. His shirts and collars were white, his suits well fitted, and his silk ties were always adorned with a pearl tie pin.

Chapman personally was not a demonstrative man. Indeed, those who knew him found him a shy man who was reluctant to talk about himself. But in the pulpit he was a powerful preacher. He commanded attention while preaching with the strength of his voice, the depth of his convictions, and the power of his illustrations. He was not in the least theatrical, but his self-confidence and sophisticated demeanor brought instant attention and lasting respect.

Chapman was searching for a full-time assistant when he met Billy Sunday. Among the qualities he sought were a willingness to work hard and travel extensively. What Chapman needed was an advance man to go into the towns ahead of him and pave the way and then to stay on during the meeting to superintend those thousands of details that were part of a well-organized program. To these qualities Chapman added some other requirements: the man must have an evangelist's heart, he must be willing and able to do some evangelistic preaching, and he must be a Bible-believing conservative who would stand his ground against the rising tide of liberalism.

After praying about his assistant, and after meeting many prospective and eager candidates, Chapman concluded that Billy Sunday was the man for the job. The Christian Association worker had fire in his soul, his energy was unbounded—indeed he was working from 8 A.M. to 10 P.M. six days a week by 1893—and he was theologically conservative. Furthermore Chapman learned that he was hurting financially. The YMCA's donations were down because of the depression, and salaries were in arrears.

Once more Billy and Ma Sunday found themselves on their knees seeking God's direction. This time, however, the answer was not so agonizing financially. The Christian Association was unable to meet its salary obligations, and the Sundays had two children to feed. Furthermore leaving the YMCA to assist J. Wilbur Chapman was hardly dereliction of duty. And Chapman's offer of $40.00 per week amounted to almost $600 a year more than he would earn at the Y, assuming they were able to pay him what they promised.

What slowed Billy Sunday from jumping at Chapman's offer was the thought of traveling again. Even though he had worked fourteen hours a day from 1891 through 1893, at least he had been able to be home with Nell every night, and he saw the children early in the morning and all day on Sunday. The prospect of frequent travel and living out of a suitcase brought back haunting memories. During his baseball days, he had missed Nell something fierce—almost to the point of despair. Could he go on the road again and find peace? Neither he nor Nell was sure.

Ultimately it became an issue of sacrifice. Was Billy Sunday willing to forsake wife, children, and the comforts of home to follow Christ's call? Everything pointed to joining up with Chapman. Only the old demon insecurity stood between what he and Nell finally perceived as his duty.

In early 1894 Billy Sunday closed another door in his life and stepped out once more on faith. Terminating a three-year stint with the YMCA, he embarked on a new career with J. Wilbur Chapman. Serving as Chapman's advance man, his duties were legion. He went ahead to the cities where Chapman was scheduled to preach, arranging housing, setting up prayer groups, organizing choirs, and tending to last-minute details. William T. Ellis, who knew both of the Sundays, recorded that "when tents were used, he would help erect them with his own hands." The new assistant "sold the evangelist's song books and sermons at meetings." He helped take up the offerings, and "when need arose, [he] spoke from the platform."

For the next twenty-three months Billy Sunday traveled the Midwest with J. Wilbur Chapman, assisting with meetings in small towns in Iowa and in Illinois communities such as Paris and Peoria. In Indiana they held crusades in Terre Haute, Richmond, Evansville, and Indianapolis. They ventured as far north as Gault, Ontario, and then eastward to Huntingdon, Pennsylvania, and Troy, New York.

During this period of extensive travel, the assistant to the Rev. Chapman was learning that there was more to doing crusade evangelistic work than just preaching. He learned how to do advance work with local pastors. Chapman had been a local pastor, and he knew something about the clergy's needs. He earned their backing by listening to their problems, discerning their foibles and needs, and then doing all possible to encourage and help them. Most of the clergy needed some time and attention themselves. They were, in effect, a group of pastors in need of a pastor. What Sunday learned early on was that the evangelistic meetings were inextricably tied to the local churches; they were successful only when seen as extensions of these local bodies. If the pastors were ministered to, encouraged, and revived spiritually themselves, they in turn could inspire their churches to unite with other churches and seek spiritual renewal within their ranks. From there they could reach out and confront nonchurched people with Christ's claims and promises and then follow that up with prayer for growing churches, more dedicated members, and a morally transformed community.

Billy Sunday also learned much about preaching during this period. Listening night after night to J. Wilbur Chapman was a rich and unique experience. No semester-long seminary course in homiletics could have matched sitting next to one of America's greatest preachers for two years, and then hearing this veteran's critique of his own tentative tries at evangelistic preaching. Chapman was a good teacher and a helpful critic. He provided Billy with texts and outlines, and he showed him how to put an effective message together. From Chapman Sunday learned to make his messages biblical and relevant. He presented the claims and promises of Christ clearly, he always called people to a decision about Christ's call on their lives, and he challenged them to become obedient to Christ's teachings. Reports from local newspapers in 1894 and 1895 made it clear that Billy Sunday was learning his lessons well. Numerous journalistic accounts of these early meetings survive, and it is obvious that local observers found Sunday's sermons to be well organized, understandable, and effective. New converts were won to the faith, and errant Christians rededicated their lives to a more faithful life.

The press clippings show not only that Billy Sunday was gaining skills from Chapman but that he was eagerly embraced by the crowds because he had his own winning style. Indeed, one of the keys to Sunday's success in the pulpit was his ability to take instruction from an able mentor and yet avoid becoming so imitative that his own personality and originality were lost in the process.

Reproductions of first-rate originals never make their own marks. And it is apparent from the surviving evidence that no one saw Sunday as a Chapman clone. An Indiana reporter noted the following about an early meeting in Evansville:

Evans Hall was packed full last night with an expectant audience, ready to see the result of the first of the Chapman meetings, which are now upon us. A choir of two hundred voices occupied seats upon the platform, and gave a song service, while on an extension platform in front were seated the city pastors and Mr. Sunday, who was the speaker of the evening.

In his unconventional and original way of putting things he is unreportable. He goes straight to the point in a most practical way that is all his own, bringing out his points with telling illustrations, and clinching them with original sayings that keep you from forgetting.

"The Bible is a commonsense Book," he said, "for it

shows man where he stands. The fact that there is joy in heaven over a repentant sinner shows that it must be an awful thing to be lost. It also shows that heaven takes an interest in men, and there is great joy there whenever a sinner is saved, because they know how great his peril has been."

He closed with an earnest prayer, and then while the Christians stood with bowed heads, he invited those who wanted to be, to raise their hands. In response to this, hands were lifted all over the house, and an after meeting was held.

A Paris, Illinois, editor was equally enthusiastic. He noted that large turnouts were forthcoming at the Christian Church in the morning and the Presbyterian Church in the afternoon. "Mr. Sunday was the leader at both places. It is evident that his baseball energy has been transferred to his new calling, for he is so much in earnest that his vitality shows in every sentence." The writer said that eighteen hundred people showed up at the tent that evening expecting Dr. Chapman to preach, but a train accident prevented his arrival, so Sunday stood in.

He had the attention of everybody, and at once demonstrated that he was quite as efficient with the Bible as with the bat. He based what he had to say on the story of the rich young man, as given in Mark 10:17-22. He had come running to Jesus, and kneeling before him, said: "What shall I do, that I may inherit eternal life?" and then went sadly away, when his question was answered in such an unexpected way. "We never know what a man is worth," said Mr. Sunday, "until after he has been tested. Those who have most of self-confidence are often the first to break down as this young fellow did. The test proves the real strength of a man, for no man is any stronger than he is at his weakest point. There was nothing unreasonable about what was required of this rich young man. God goes halvers on nothing, but demands all.

"No girl would be willing to marry a young man who

would only promise to give her a little of his love. She must
have it all, and so it is with God. He must be loved with
the whole heart. With an undivided heart, and right there
is where the young moneybags in the lesson fell down. He
cared more for his ducats than he did for Christ, and that
is what lost him his soul. God has every right to demand
our very best. It would have been no harder for the young
man to give up all he had than for Abraham to give up his
friends, his home and his native land. Peter left his boat
and fishing nets—all he had—to follow Christ, and every
Christian worth his salt does the same, and so must you
and I."

Sunday's apprenticeship with Chapman obviously helped
him in his preaching and his organizational skills, and apparently it also taught him to dress well. An Iowa newspaper
reporter remarked that "He does not look like a preacher. He
would more likely be taken for a speculator on the stock exchange, or a prematurely old young business man. But when he
. . . launches out into his sermon, you stop thinking about the
man, and have to think of what he is saying, and when he is
through you know you have been listening to a genius divinely
crowned."

Chapman may have taught Billy to dress well, but he did
not encourage an appetite for a materialistic lifestyle in other
ways. In fact, Chapman downplayed finances and put little
emphasis on fund-raising. They took up a collection, to be sure,
but he placed no pressure on the listeners to give. On the
contrary, he avoided paying attention to money, trusting God
to provide a modest salary for himself and his staff workers.
Billy Sunday's correspondence indicates that Chapman, a married man since 1882, lived frugally and simply. His idea of the
good life was getting away to be with his wife and perhaps
spending a few days or weeks in a cottage at Winona Lake in
Indiana. That Chapman never lined his own pockets in any way
was common knowledge, and it is demonstrated by the fact that
although he purchased a vacation house on Winona Lake in the

last years of the nineteenth century, he purchased it on time. And in December 1908 he offered to sell it to the Sundays, who were—thanks to Chapman—in love with this Indiana lake and countryside. By then at the peak of his career, Chapman explained that he could not afford to keep the property, and he still owed $1,500 on the mortgage.

Chapman had learned to trust God's provisions rather than mammon. Markedly influenced by the deeper-life movement in Keswick, England, he credited Britain's F. B. Meyer as well as America's Dwight L. Moody with helping him learn to lean on the Holy Spirit rather than the things of this world. In this vein, Chapman wrote a book entitled *Received Ye the Holy Ghost?* Published in 1894, this book helped turn Billy Sunday's eyes from the world's treasures and enabled him to focus more clearly on the resurrected Christ. A significant manifestation of this influence was the young evangelist's serious commitment to prayer, which was so evident to those around him that he and Helen were eventually in great demand to speak at conferences on the subject of prayer.

No doubt this devotion to a deeper spiritual life was one of the most important contributions Chapman made to Sunday's life and ministry. Beyond this, however, he helped reinforce Billy's commitment to conservative biblical Christianity. Some liberals argued that the best educated and most sophisticated preachers had moved beyond Scripture to rely more on reason and experience, but Sunday had evidence to the contrary. J. Wilbur Chapman was one of the best educated clergyman in America. He had studied in two renowned institutions and had earned three degrees, including a prestigious doctorate. All who knew him attested to Dr. Chapman's brilliance. He possessed a first-rate mind, and he used it critically, analytically, and judiciously. In short, if the poorly educated Sunday was tempted to be intimidated by more poised and lettered liberals, he had been and would continue to be encouraged in responsible conservatism by Chapman—a man Sunday believed was without peer.

Clearly Chapman was important in Billy's life, and when he made a momentous decision during their winter break in November and December 1895, it affected the Sundays deeply. Chapman routinely received calls from churches to come and serve as their pastor. At this time he received a special call to return to his former pastorate at a large and influential church in Philadelphia. Wrestling with the unexpected call, this faithful man took the issue to prayer. Without ever consulting Billy Sunday or anyone else but Mrs. Chapman, the eminent evangelist made his decision to return to the church and resume his pastoral duties. Billy Sunday remembered it this way: "We separated for our homes for the holidays, and while we were getting ready for a Christmas celebration for our children, Helen and George, who were little tots then, Doctor Chapman wired me that he had decided to quit evangelistic work and had accepted the pastorate of the Bethany Presbyterian Church."

Billy and Nell were stunned. What was going on? What was God's plan for their lives now? Could they have misunderstood the Lord's call when they decided to join up with Chapman two years before? "There I was, out of work," Sunday reminisced. "I had a wife and two children to support." Should he go back to professional baseball? No. He was called to evangelistic ministry. Besides, he had been away from the sport too many years to get back now. Should he try to go back to the YMCA? As usual, Billy and Nell "laid it before the Lord." They were beginning to realize that God does not give his people a life free of adversity, that he rather calls them to perseverance and faith.

"Faith," observed the unemployed preacher, "is the beginning of something of which you can't see the end but in which you believe."

The Sundays went on with Christmas as planned. And they waited. According to Nell's recollections, "another telegram came six days after we received Dr. Chapman's, and it was from a man who said, 'A Methodist preacher, a Baptist preacher, and I have united, and we're going to hold a revival in our town of Garner, Iowa.' He said, 'We've rented the Opera House already, and we'd like to know whether you will come to lead us in our revival.' " Ma recalled that she and Billy were numb, then ecstatic.

> Would he go! It was just as if that telegram were sent like manna from heaven—just like food to a starving man. I remember being so happy about it, and I put my arms around Billy's neck and I hung on so tightly that I dragged him to the carpet. We both had a great laugh together over our joy at getting the telegram. And, of course, I went right away to send the word, "Yes!"

Billy recalled that he "didn't know anybody out there, and I don't know yet why they ever asked me to hold meetings. But I went." He opened his own evangelistic meetings on January 7, 1896, in little Garner, Iowa, a town in the north central part of the state about forty miles below the Minnesota line. It was in this farm-service community of approximately one thousand people that he launched a preaching ministry that would last until his death. Before he had finished a week of services at Garner, Billy was asked to go down to a town about twice Garner's size, Sigourney, located in southeastern Iowa about fifty miles above the Missouri state line. Sigourney's pastors asked the Iowa-born evangelist to preach in their town from January 19 through the first week of February. Neither he nor the men who invited him had any idea that this trip back to Iowa was the beginning of a career and a calling that would last almost four decades, would take him to America's great cities, and would vault him to national fame.

In truth, the train trip to Iowa in January 1896 marked the end of Billy Sunday's apprenticeship. But he had no inkling of this. Indeed, there was neither evidence nor premonition to suggest that these Iowa meetings were a prelude to an illustrious preaching career. Although he would never again be without an invitation to preach, and neither he nor his family would ever have to miss a meal again, there were financial trials and enormous personal tribulations ahead. For Sunday, though, there was no glimpse of the future. His task was to walk a day and a week at a time.

4 The Kerosene Circuit

1896-1907

"One hundred more converted yesterday. God is moving surely."

There was absolutely nothing glamorous about the next twelve years of Billy Sunday's life. Anyone who thinks he entered evangelistic ministry for ease of life, to earn lots of money, to travel to exotic places, or to enjoy fawning crowds knows nothing about the early years of his work. Between January 1896 and November 1907 the Iowa-born resident of Chicago preached in approximately seventy different communities. Of the sixty-six documented revivals, twenty-eight were in Iowa and twenty-four in Illinois. Three engagements were held in southern Nebraska, five in southern Minnesota, one in northern Missouri, and two in southern Indiana. Only three engagements in over a decade were in anything close to resort-like places—two in Colorado and one in Woodstock, New York. The eastern location was indeed a lovely retreat center in the Catskills, but he was there for only a few days. The Colorado towns were hardly on the tourist trail. Canon City was the home of the state penitentiary, located on a rather barren landscape near the ascending Rockies. And Salida, Colorado, was an Arkansas River valley agricultural town bereft of the tourists who descended on such spots as Pike's Peak, Colorado Springs, or Estes Park.

Billy Sunday, a resident of up-to-date Chicago since the early 1880s, referred to these towns as being on "The Kerosene Circuit." Neither natural gas nor electric lights adorned such places. Indeed, although the bulk of these agricultural-service communities were located along the railroad lines, mostly they were villages with populations in four figures (usually 1,000-7,000); only four had more than ten thousand residents. The largest two were in Illinois—Peoria with 56,000 and Rockford at 30,000.

Sunday traveled from one midwestern community to another by railway coach. It was uncomfortable sitting in chair cars, where the seats were upright and hard. In warm weather the windows stayed open, and the traveler was slowly coated with prairie dust and soot from the engine. In cold weather the windows stayed closed, but the drafty doors leaked and the cold floors creaked. It was almost impossible to sleep in the chairs, which transmitted every bump and clank of the wheels. Sleeping was difficult enough on pre–World War I trains even in first-class Pullman sleeping cars—which Sunday could not afford in any case. He sat upright, read his Bible, worked on sermon outlines, and dozed as best he could between whistle stops.

In those early years the young evangelist mapped his schedule only a few weeks in advance. While speaking in one town he might receive a telegram from another community asking him to come to them as soon as possible. Likewise it was not unusual, especially in the 1890s, for an itinerary to develop in this way: he was in Mills County in southwestern Iowa, delivering a series of services over several nights in Emerson. Visitors from nearby Tabor would hear that the evangelist was in the county, and after checking him out they would invite him to their village fifteen miles away as the crow flies, but a bit farther by horse and buggy along the farm-to-market roads. No sooner would the word get out that he was speaking in Emerson and slated for Tabor than a delegation from Malvern, not to be outdone by their county neighbors, would be on hand to extend an invitation to their town as well.

In those early years the meetings were usually in local churches, but most of those buildings held only one or two hundred people. If a town hall that seated several hundred to a thousand people was available, the churches and civic leaders would often pool their resources and rent the facility to accommodate a larger crowd. Even the largest available buildings in these small communities were fairly small, however; if an evangelist like Billy Sunday wanted to reach large numbers of people, he had to travel from one town to another.

Gradually, however, Sunday started to attract larger crowds, and to accommodate them he began renting tents during his spring, summer, and fall campaigns. The big canvas tents, complete with three center poles, heavy ropes, and enormous stakes, had the advantage of seating more people than available fixed structures; during warm weather, the side flaps could be raised and people could sit outside. But they had significant drawbacks as well. Prairie winds would cause the poles to sway and the flaps to pop. If the weather was warm and the side flaps were up, the congregation was exposed to all manner of distractions on the outside. Even with the flaps down and under the best of conditions, noises and other distractions in those days before microphones made it difficult for the evangelist to make himself heard. Add to these problems heat in the summer, cold in the autumn, and dust always—on the floor, in the air, on the notes, and all over one's clothes—and it is clear that tent services were far from ideal.

During the first decade or so of his ministry, before he made a name for himself, it remained Billy's responsibility to hire a tent, erect it, and see to its security. Letters home during the late 1890s show that the itinerant evangelist spent no small amount of time driving stakes into the ground, erecting poles, and securing tent ropes. Bitter experience taught him that heavy rains or winds would bring his canvas tabernacles to the ground unless a strong hand was available to tighten or loosen ropes as the conditions required. After one or two devastating storms, Sunday took to sleeping in the tents when inclement weather was forecast. When the storms hit, he would run from place to place like a sailor on deck during a storm, adjusting the rigging to prevent a total collapse. When weather was less threatening, the young preacher usually stayed in a local hotel or rooming house, and the wives of local preachers and deacons fed him heaping plates of fried chicken, potatoes, and gravy. He burned up the calories of those meals in the early days not only by preaching furiously but also through the sheer physical effort of keeping his tents standing.

It was not until 1905 that Billy could afford to hire an assistant evangelist to travel with him. Nearly ten years after Sunday went to Garner, Iowa, for his first independent revival, he asked Fred Siebert to be his aide—to do some advance work, erect the tents, watch the facilities at night, and do some preaching. But shortly after Sunday hired the "Cowboy Evangelist," as Siebert was known in the Midwest, the powerful newcomer was relieved of the onerous task of raising and watching the tent. During Sunday's month-long series of services in Salida, Colorado, in 1906, their tent was destroyed and the meetings shut down. When the Billy Sunday team arrived on September 20, the weather was beautiful. The skies were blue, the days warm, and the nights cool and dry. But after four weeks of good weather, an unexpected snowstorm blanketed the town while everyone slept. Early the next morning the townspeople awakened to four or five inches of heavy, wet snow. Leaf-covered branches were broken from trees, and the revivalist's tent collapsed under the weight.

Their tent demolished, Sunday and Siebert said good-bye to Colorado for the season and returned to Illinois. The experience also led Sunday to make a permanent change in his ministry. From October 1906 on he avoided tent meetings. If the churches or town halls could not hold the congregations, Sunday insisted that a wooden tabernacle be constructed at the community's expense. If the civic leaders and preachers could not provide a lot and building, then he turned down the opportunity and selected from the increasingly large number of other invitations he was receiving.

Of course Billy Sunday was no stranger to wooden tabernacles. Both J. Wilbur Chapman and Dwight L. Moody had used such structures in the early 1890s, and Billy himself had persuaded a few towns to erect buildings for him after the turn of the century. Perry, Iowa, a town of just under four thousand residents, erected the first Billy Sunday tabernacle in 1901. It was a relatively costly enterprise, but offerings were good enough to pay the cost, and the building was torn down and the lumber sold once the meetings concluded.

Using a tabernacle in 1901 certainly did not solve all of the problems associated with a campaign, but it did provide a number of benefits. First of all it was a status symbol for Billy Sunday, a sign that like Moody and Chapman before him he had arrived. Tabernacles also served as good publicity for the communities that constructed them. In those days towns competed fiercely with one another for the limelight. It was important to civic leaders that they be the first in their region to adopt up-to-date programs and projects. In the little wars for regional dominance, being the first to have Billy Sunday speak or the first to erect a tabernacle put them on the map. To some of the local elite, this element of civic pride was as important as anything the evangelist might do or say.

Sadly, it would seem that the disease of pride that infected some of the towns that built tabernacles spread to local preachers and to Billy Sunday himself. He began by merely urging towns to build tabernacles. Several communities followed the lead of Perry, Iowa, after 1901. But, as noted, after the Salida snowstorm in 1906, he made it a condition for his coming. Moreover, once a commitment was made to construct a tabernacle, the controversial issue of money appeared. It was a relatively minor matter to rent a town hall, and when he was using such facilities, Billy never asked for more than a freewill offering on the last night of his revival. But building a wooden structure that held several hundred or a thousand people was another matter. Business and civic leaders would have to put up the money in advance for materials and labor, and this amounted to considerably more than what it cost to rent a tent. It was assumed that the congregations would make sufficient contributions to pay for these temporary wooden meeting halls, but if the donations were not forthcoming, a local committee was stuck with the tab.

The very existence of this financial problem added a new dimension to Sunday's work. Both he and the local preachers who invited him now felt a pressure to raise funds or encourage large offerings. It was not a big issue in these early years, because the tabernacles were relatively small and simple. And the testimonial letters from towns where Sunday preached prior to 1908 frequently stressed the fact that he never asked for money. But as the years went by and increasingly larger tabernacles and more elaborate acoustics were required, the issue of money became more prominent, and it did not enhance the evangelist's image or glorify his work.

To be sure, the tabernacles did some good things for Sunday's ministry. Most notably, they enabled him to hold larger meetings during the winter. In many areas of the country cold weather made it impossible to hold tent revivals from Thanksgiving to Easter. And it is also true that the construction of a tabernacle made for good publicity. It was such a remarkable event in middle America that it made front page news in local and regional newspapers, vaulting Sunday into more prominence and leading to yet more invitations to preach. In short, building tabernacles and having Billy Sunday was gradually becoming the fashion.

Billy's ministry enjoyed another benefit from the construction of tabernacles as well—at least in the few places they were raised in the early years, 1901 to 1906. During that period, the need for such structures was making the evangelist better known, but it had not yet made him so important that he did not have to do some of the work. His letters to Nell indicate that he spent plenty of hours helping raise buildings and tar roofs. His participation in this hard work made the people love Billy Sunday. He might dress like a Chicago banker when he first came to town and whenever he stepped into the pulpit, but what these country people liked about the preacher who was himself reared between the plow handles was that he would also put on work clothes, climb ladders, and hammer nails with the rest of the men.

During those first years of the new century Billy went to towns that were relatively poor. They might have metropolitan aspirations, but they had not yet arrived. It was one thing for them to agree to build a tabernacle, but quite another for them to find the necessary money for labor and material. It happened more than once that the task was accomplished only through a donation of community effort. Sunday and the local preachers would join farmers and townspeople in raising the tabernacle. The women would bring food, the men would put up the structure, and often a baseball game would be played after the serious work of building and eating was done. That Sunday would join in these enterprises immensely pleased the towns-folk and went miles toward building rapport. He had, after all, lived in rural Iowa for over twenty years. He had done their kind of work, he knew the strain of their toil, and he enjoyed their idea of a feast. Once the work was done, he warmed their hearts by mingling among the people. He learned some of their names, he listened to their problems, and he broke bread and ate chicken with them on the grass. The local preachers especially valued the opportunity to get to know the evangelist and tell him of their joys and cares. And everyone, particularly the young, was thrilled when the former professional baseball player would run back to his room, slip into his major league uniform, and challenge everyone to a few innings of play.

To these people in Iowa, Illinois, western Nebraska, southern Minnesota, and Indiana, Billy Sunday was the "baseball Evangelist," and he was one of them. Their towns, with average populations of 1,500 to 4,000, were built by people who knew farming as a way of life. These communities were surrounded by farms, their livelihood depended upon farming, and most of the residents had done some farming before coming to town when the railroad came and opened up new economic opportunities. Most of these folks were born in America. If they were not native to the Midwest, they came from states to the east. Of the immigrants and children of immigrants among the middle border dwellers, most had come from northern and western Europe (Britain, Scandinavia, the Netherlands, or Germany). Like Billy Sunday most of these folks had been exposed to Christianity of a Protestant variety, and they had relocated more than once or twice seeking greater economic gain. There were among them a few people who had become fairly rich, and in their orbit of life they were men and women of status and power. Many more were simply getting by passably well. They never missed any meals, and if crop yields were good, world markets favorable, and the national economy strong, they experienced a gradual climb up the social scale by adding a room to their house or purchasing some new furniture and some ready-made clothes.

This is not to say that they didn't know hardship. Life expectancy was not above age sixty in most states, and infant mortality was extremely high. Medical care was poor or nonexistent, and almost everyone suffered from some chronic malady which was treated with herbs or patent medicines. The Civil War had brought pain to the majority of families, and veterans of the great conflict were present in every crowd. The marks of that cruel war were evident everywhere—in damaged emotions and damaged bodies. The depressions of the 1870s and 1890s had hurt countless families. Many had lost their land when market prices or crop failures prevented them from meeting mortgage payments. Sunday identified with all of this. His father died in the Civil War, he lived through the two depressions, and he watched the twin enemies of death and poverty unleash their blows on his family and neighbors.

But Billy did more than identify with these people's pains; he also shared their expectations. He, too, had left the farm and gone to the city in search of lucrative work and respite from the drudgery of farm labor. Like them he did not hate rural America; he just wanted to be free of the whims of nature and the back-breaking, never-ending work. And while he aspired as they did to the comforts and advantages of big city life, he knew that the Garners, Perrys, Marshalls, and Maryvilles were not yet metropolises and they were not likely to be. Like these midwestern Americans, he at once admired the successful big-city people and disliked them for looking down their noses at farmers and small-town people. Billy Sunday and the folks he preached to still held rural America and all it stood for in high regard. And if many of them did not fully embrace the Jeffersonian "lord of the soil" image for farmers, they certainly did not assume with big-city dwellers that ruralites were bumpkins, hayseeds, and rubes.

Because Billy Sunday shared the perspective of these many middle Americans who were still on the farm, had just left it, or were at most a few years or a half generation away, he was marvelously successful in reaching them. He not only thought their way and shared their worldview, but he spoke their language. He could always draw appreciative laughter with his down-home delivery. "The man who can drive a hog and keep his religion will stand without hitching," he would say, or, "You don't have to look like a hedgehog to be pious." The average seminary-trained theologian might not have fully appreciated Billy's bellowing that "You can find everything in the average church from a hummingbird to a turkey buzzard," but it went down well in western Nebraska and most of Iowa.

Peppering his sermons with country phrases and witticisms attracted the audience's attention. When this was added to the goodwill he had engendered by mixing with the people and getting to know them, he had them ready to listen to the burden of his heart—the serious theme of his message. Billy believed that he was God's messenger. He was convinced that Isaiah 61:1 ("The Spirit of the Lord God is upon me; because the Lord hath anointed me to preach good tidings unto the meek; he hath sent me to bind up the brokenhearted, to proclaim liberty to the captives, and the opening of the prisons to them that are bound") applied personally to him and his divine call. And he believed that his message was the most important any man, woman, or child could receive. He was certain that no one could enter into eternal life without faith in Jesus Christ. He assumed every person would die, face judgment, and then spend eternity in either heaven or hell, depending solely upon his or her relationship to Christ. In brief, all people have sinned, and all sinners are doomed. But the good news, which Sunday was called to announce to all who would listen, is that Jesus died for sinners. All those who confess their sins, ask for forgiveness, allow Christ to be Lord of their life, and choose to follow Christ and serve him will be saved, will lead a better life now, and will spend eternity in heaven.

Faith in Christ was what Sunday preached, not church membership. "Going to church don't make anybody a Christian," he said, "any more than taking a wheelbarrow into a garage makes it an automobile. . . . No hypocrite in the church, or out of it, is going to get into heaven." He warned that following him would not get them to heaven either. Indeed, "if you follow some of the star preachers you will be lost in the woods, but if you follow Christ you will be sure to land in heaven." This is typically the message he laid before the people:

Years ago, Jesus came to take up his abode in my heart and life. I am honored. He is my guest, and will be until the end.
1. I believe that the Lord Jesus Christ died for me.
2. I have accepted Him as my Savior.
3. I have confessed Him before the world.
4. I trust Him from day to day.

Sunday noted that most people felt they were not functioning as well as they should—they had dark sins and secrets that made them feel guilty, they were locked into habits they could not break, their relationships with others were broken or hurtful, they were unsettled inside, and they were afraid to die. "What can be done?" he asked. "Here is a watch. It does not run. Would you say, 'Give it new surroundings?' No, you'd say, 'Give it a new mainspring.'" The new mainspring, of course, enables it to work again—the way its maker designed it. Then he talked about the new mainspring that had totally revived and changed his own life.

> I know salvation has done three things for me:
> 1. It has made me a happier man.
> 2. It has made me a better man.
> 3. It has made me more useful.

In this vein the evangelist called people to get right with God through Christ, to be assured of eternal life in heaven, and to live a fuller, more productive life here and now. "Surrender to Christ and stop drinking up your paycheck. . . . Get right with God and spend more time with your wife and children. . . . Follow Christ and earn money for your family by doing an honest day's work. . . . Become a Christian and stop using tobacco. . . . Be Christ's man and do more with your life than play cards and dance."

Yet Billy Sunday did more than challenge non-Christians to repent and follow Christ into new lives; he also called upon believers to be revived.

Some critics have accused Sunday of pharisaical legalism because he ranted against the immorality of Christians and heathens alike, but this misses the mark. He was saddened and angered by the spectacle of people who called themselves Christians but who were just as materialistic, just as addicted to alcohol, and just as debased by sexual immorality as the people who never professed faith in Christ. He felt compelled to warn them of the danger they faced by continuing in sin. And yet in his calls to repentance he never slighted the fact that it is a loving God who calls his wandering children to repent and be saved.

71

Sunday was markedly influenced by England's Keswick movement—a spiritual renewal program that began in England's Lake District in the 1870s. Keswick teaching was directed to Christians—Christians who were continually defeated by sin and thereby incapable of improving their lives. The "sin-sick" Christians, according to Keswick teachers (among whom was F. B. Meyer, who greatly influenced Sunday's mentor J. Wilbur Chapman), were indistinguishable from heathens, were defeated to the point of being unable to serve Christ in ministry, in the home, at work, or on the mission field.

Put another way, Billy Sunday knew personally what it was like to be in bondage to sin. He spent much energy calling unbelievers out of their chains through Christ, but he also believed that many Christians were as seriously bound—and he believed that Christians could *choose* to be free. Although he never expressed it in a theologically sophisticated manner, Sunday was convinced of the possibility and desirability of sanctification. He got this, in part, from Chapman and the Keswick teachers. He also got a strong dose of it from E. M. Bounds, a Wesleyan holiness author and evangelist whose books greatly touched the self-educated evangelist.

Sunday also believed that many churches were losing members and dying because believers had been listening to liberal preachers—he called them "modernists"—who doubted the truth of the Bible. Sunday frequently said, "Nowadays we think we are too smart to believe in the Virgin birth of Jesus, and too well educated to believe in the resurrection." Such sophistication was "why people are going to the devil in multitudes." His sermons were laden with exhortations to trust the Bible because it "tells us of our only hope. The Bible is, or is not, the Word of God. If God did not inspire men to write it, then He has never made a revelation to us. . . . All we know about heaven and salvation is in the Bible." He emphasized the point that, contrary to liberal opinion, "God is not discovered; He is revealed."

Sunday also exhorted believers to pray—and to return to

faith in prayer. "Prayer is beginning to be looked upon as old-fashioned. People are not praying today." In company with Wesleyan holiness people and Keswick "deeper-life" adherents, he declared that "God answers prayer."

Abraham prayed for a son, and God gave him a posterity like the sands of the sea. He prayed for Ishmael; God spared the boy's life, and made of him a great nation.

He prayed for Sodom; God heard his prayer, and postponed the day of doom.

Jacob prayed for a favorable reception for Esau.

Moses prayed for the forgiveness of the people.

Gideon prayed God to overthrow the Midianites.

Elijah prayed, and God heard and answered by fire.

Joshua prayed, Achan was discovered.

Hannah prayed, and Samuel was born.

Hezekiah prayed, and 185,000 Assyrians died.

Daniel prayed, and the lions were muzzled.

The Apostles prayed, and the Holy Spirit came down.

Not one of these things would have happened without prayer.

Luther prayed, and the Reformation was the result.

Knox prayed, and Scotland trembled.

Brainerd prayed, and the Indians were subdued.

Wesley prayed, and millions moved Godward.

Whitfield prayed, and thousands were converted.

Finney prayed, and mighty revivals resulted.

Taylor prayed, and the great China Inland Mission was born.

Mueller prayed, and more than seven million dollars were sent to him to feed thousands of orphans.

Auntie Cook prayed; Moody was anointed, and the Moody Bible Institute was launched.

We are always praying; God is always answering.

Billy Sunday preached such words as these in scores of towns all over the Midwest from 1896 to 1907. Assuming he was God's messenger fulfilling the Great Commission of Jesus to "go into all the world and preach the gospel," he called for people to repent, turn from their lives of sin, and find new life—eternal life—by trusting in Christ and obeying his commands. Sunday also urged indolent church members to repent—to get back into Bible study and apply its teaching to their daily lives. He also called people to a life of prayer, and he urged believers to give up the worldly pleasures of alcohol, tobacco, dancing, and card playing. Christians, he preached, were called to be holy. They did not have to wallow in the bondage of life-destroying habits. Christ had paid their penalty for sin, and he had also provided for their sanctification.

Pointing unbelievers to Jesus Christ and exhorting backsliding believers to a renewed commitment to discipleship were his main goals. And when he finished a message he left the pulpit and stood down in the front of the platform. While a hymn was played on an organ or piano, he asked people to come forward—to come and take his hand and say "I am a sinner but I want to follow Christ," or "I am an errant believer and I want to renew my commitment to be a disciple of Christ."

By the tens, scores, and eventually hundreds they came forward. They walked down the dusty pathways in tents or on the rickety floors of town halls. Some with smiles on their faces, others with tears in their eyes, they whispered their first-time or renewed Christian commitment to the imploring preacher. This was the highlight of every meeting for Billy Sunday. Without fail he wrote to Nell and told her what had transpired. In one little town only "109 came out." But when a few came forward it was worth every minute of his time. He was especially elated, his letters show, when the halls were full and the decision makers were many. Indeed, from Colorado he wrote "they are beginning to break 150 to 200 a night," and from a great plains state he elatedly wrote "100 more converted yesterday. God is moving surely."

Growing crowds and the subsequent need to search for larger facilities after a few nights in a town always encouraged the evangelist. Likewise the hundreds of conversions—over one thousand in early 1905 in Dixon, Illinois, for example, and over six hundred in Redwood Falls, Minnesota, earlier—were balm to this tired man. He was also pleased to learn that regular church attendance increased in the wake of his revivals, and saloons—sometimes several in one town—lost so much business that they were forced to close. The traveling preacher was thrilled, too, when weeks, months, and even years after his services he received mail from those who came forward and shook his hand, testifying to how they had stopped drinking after years of addiction or how marriages had been saved, how guilt had been lifted, lives rebuilt, and peace of mind experienced. Sometimes the testimonials contained a small contribution, urging him to use, as one woman put it, "my widow's mite" to help his family. Occasionally the letters were from family members who wanted Sunday to know that a husband, a wife, a son, or a daughter had been spectacularly transformed because of his preaching; and a few epistles heartened the preacher with reports of how an entire town had been reformed and stabilized through his ministry.

All of these evidences of change encouraged Billy and kept him on the trail, but few things pleased him more than some belated recognition from fellow clergy. To be sure, the local preachers who invited him loved him, and those whose churches grew in his wake were congratulatory and fulsome in their praise. But it was not until 1898 that the Presbyterian Church bestowed a formal license to preach on this thirty-six-year-old man who had been preaching with marked success for several years. In those days licensing meant that the denomination recognized that the preacher had ministerial gifts and that he was being considered for formal ordination. The licensee was certified to preach, but he was not deemed worthy of full ordination with all of its rights and privileges.

Becoming licensed bolstered Billy Sunday's personal esteem, but it paled in comparison to the ordination which came in 1903. Sunday did not need ordination to do the work of an evangelist. In fact, Dwight L. Moody had refused offers of ordination on the grounds that God ordained what he was doing and that credentials required for pastoral ministries were not important for his calling. But to Billy Sunday ordination—recognition by his peers and the concomitant right to the title "Reverend"—constituted a crucial symbol of acceptance and success. It should be remembered that Billy was always an insecure man. The death of his father, his years in an orphanage, his lack of formal schooling, his self-consciousness at being an unpolished hick in Chicago's world of sophistication, and his difficulty in winning acceptance from Nell's urbane family all conspired to give him fits of self-doubt and agony. Without the encouragement of Nell—without her enormous confidence in his innate ability and her surety of God's call on his life—it is doubtful that he would have been a successful preacher. His letters to Nell reveal that he frequently suffered self-doubt, discouragement, and depression. It was "Ma," as he lovingly called her, who could pick him up, convince him he had great worth, and remind him of God's call on his life. From this perspective, it is clear that while ordination may not have been necessary as a professional seal of approval, it was personally edifying.

Some historians have treated his ordination as a joke. No doubt Sunday himself contributed to this interpretation when thirty years later, in the relative security of established fame, he poked fun at himself and his own ignorance. He recalled his ordination exam this way:

> Professor Zenos, of McCormick Theological Seminary . . . asked me about St. Augustine, [and] I replied, "He didn't play in the National League, I don't know him." So I muffed the first ball he threw at me. I tried to steal second, but they caught me between bases. The umpire, Dr. Herrick Johnson, then said, "Mr. Moderator, I move this needless examination stop. What difference does it make if he knows about Alexander, Savonarola and Cleopatra, or 'Pop' Anson? God has used him to win more souls to Christ than all of us combined, and must have ordained him long before we ever thought of it. I move that he be admitted to

the Presbytery and we give him the right hand of fellowship and the authority of the Presbyterian Church."

Perhaps that was the way the church history portion of the
examination went, and it is probably close to the way the
examination was concluded. But the truth is more complicated.
In reality Sunday had applied to the Chicago Presbytery for
ordination. He was examined by an august council of men of
integrity. Among them, besides the church historian, were Dr.
J. G. K. McClure, president of Lake Forest (Chapman's alma
mater), the pastor of Jefferson Park Presbyterian Church, and
several other demanding ministers and administrators in the
Chicago Presbytery. These men were not about to ordain a
candidate who was ignorant of Scripture or doctrinally un-
sound. Although Billy was doubtless allowed to say "I don't
know" or "That's too deep for me" or "I'll have to pass that up"
a few times, he was nonetheless required to demonstrate a
thorough knowledge of the Scriptures as well as a firm grip of
biblical and traditional Presbyterian theology and a working
knowledge of the denominational polity. In any case, the examination lasted for over an hour, and inasmuch as Sunday was not
yet a nationally renowned preacher at this time, there would
have been little pressure to pass him. On the contrary, there is
every reason to assume the candidate did well in everything but
church history—the least critical of the areas in which he was
examined. In fact, a careful study of Sunday's sermons demon-
strates that before and after his ordination he had a clear grasp
of conservative doctrine and theology. Although he joked, used
homey illustrations, and relied on barnyard metaphors, he was
no buffoon. His christology was strong, and his knowledge of
Scripture impressive.

The formal ordination service was held at Chicago's Jefferson Park Presbyterian Church, the church where Billy met Nell,
received his early Bible and discipleship instruction, and served
as an elder for many years. At the service Dr. Alexander Patterson gave the charge, and Dr. J. Wilbur Chapman preached the

ordination sermon. Chapman's rhetoric was probably different, but the spirit of his affirmation of Sunday's divine call and preparation must have been like that of Dr. R. M. Russell, president of Westminster College, New Wilmington, Pennsylvania, when he conferred an honorary doctor of divinity degree on the preacher nine years later:

> We count it to the honor of Westminster that we did this thing. Mr. Sunday knows his Bible, which is the true body of Divinity in theological lore. He has devoted his life to the supreme task of world evangelization, for which the Bible is the great charter. He is, therefore, both in scholarship and practical effort, entitled to the degree.
>
> Just as the doctor of medicine is supposed to know the science of medicine, and practice the art of healing, so a Doctor of Divinity who knows the truth about God, and practices the art of saving, is entitled to a degree. In many institutions it is customary to bestow the honorary degree of Doctor of Divinity upon those who are men more noted for their knowledge of "the traditions of the scribes and Pharisees" than for their knowledge and practical use of the Bible itself.

It was important for Billy Sunday that he now had "Reverend" before his name and ample evidence of growing attendance and converts before his eyes. Otherwise the eleven years between his first revival at Garner in 1896 and the rapid rise of stardom in larger cities beginning in 1908 might have been too pressure-laden to bear. To those who look back on Sunday's life with only a superficial glance, he left baseball and experienced a meteoric rise to prosperity and fame as a nationally celebrated evangelist. The truth is starkly different. When he left baseball in 1891 he was relatively well known as a sports figure—at least among those who followed the game. But when he went to work for the YMCA, he began slipping into obscurity. "Former" sports stars are soon forgotten—even the greats. And while Sunday was good at baseball, he was far from great. It is true that he traded on his sports reputation in the earliest days of his preaching, but in reality he went from being mentioned daily in the urban press to being recognized as a competent speaker among a small, if growing, number of people who moved in conservative Christian circles. Working for J. Wilbur Chapman left him largely in that man's shadow, and as well-known as Chapman was among conservative Christians, he was hardly a household name across America. When Sunday set out on his own after 1896, he began to make headlines in the local press, but having one's name emblazoned across a small-town weekly or even prominently displayed in the pages of an Iowa daily in a town of four thousand was not enough to attract the attention of the national wire services. Sunday was not featured in a major magazine until autumn 1907, and his name did not appear in the *New York Times* until 1909. Why? He simply was not newsworthy. He traveled hundreds of miles in a relatively small geographic area, spending ninety percent of his time in small communities in Iowa and Illinois.

There is no way to romanticize his first eleven years of ministry—nearly a third of his career as an independent preacher. The towns where he stayed had shabby hotels and rooming houses. The buildings were lighted by kerosene lamps, the streets were unpaved, and for most of that time the evangelist was so poor and unimportant that he had to help erect his own tents and tabernacles. Frequently he was broke. He would send forty dollars here and one hundred dollars there to Nell as he could, but if her father had not provided sizable monetary gifts, Billy probably could not have continued his preaching. He even experienced the embarrassment of having to ask Nell for expense money on at least one trip.

Funds were so scarce that Billy had to direct the choir himself at Garner, Iowa—a problem, because he was no musician. There is no evidence he could read music, and he evidently never played an instrument. He was so ludicrous in the song leader's role at Garner that the word went out to the next town to find a local parson to do the job. There was no money to pay a musician in the early years. It was not until 1898 that he hired his first vocalist for special music. But she and others like her were hired to perform only in the towns where they lived, not to travel with the ministry, and they were paid only a few dollars from the offering.

Renting tents and constructing tabernacles added to Sunday's living and traveling expenses, but these structures did make room for more people and larger offerings. The extra money eventually allowed Billy to hire his first regular singer and musician, Fred Fischer, a wavy-haired dandy who sported fashionable clothes, pince-nez glasses, and a big mustache with turned-up waxed ends. He joined Billy in 1900 and traveled with him until 1910. Finances had improved enough by 1905 that they added the rugged, hard-handed Fred Siebert to their group, assigning the "Cowboy Evangelist" to the role of advance man, assistant evangelist, and official tent and tabernacle custodian.

If finances were better by 1900, other issues grew worse. Liberal opposition became more marked, especially when Sunday got into larger towns and cities. Liberal preachers and some mainline pastors openly criticized Sunday's preaching, belittling his style and deploring his theology. Episcopalians and some Lutherans found his views of how one enters into a relationship with Christ to be crude if not errant. Society people objected to his presence because they disliked his style and were afraid their community would be identified with his folksy ways. Saloon keepers and liquor dealers derided him unmercifully, and some hotel owners and brothel keepers, fearing dwindling revenues, tried to silence him through disparagement and threats.

Plenty of non-Protestant religious leaders criticized Sunday as well. Some Roman Catholic churches with largely Irish or German congregations interpreted his attacks on saloon keeping and drinking as insults directed at their ethnic backgrounds. And attacks also came from some conservative church quarters—especially independent fundamentalists and Baptists—who condemned the evangelist for associating with members of secret societies such as the Masons and Woodmen of the World and who could not understand why he frequently reached out to Roman Catholics and put in a good word for them.

Always an insecure man, Sunday found criticism harder to bear than an empty wallet—although poverty was a heavy burden for a man who had tasted so much deprivation since childhood. Nevertheless, his most weighty deprivation by far was separation from Nell and the family. Billy and Nell were married in 1888, eight years before he went out on his own. Their first child, Helen, was born in 1890, and George Marquis followed shortly after in 1892. He had been home for the first six years of Helen's life and the first four of George's, but beyond this he had largely missed the joy of helping them grow up. He had been away from his family some of the time while he worked for J. Wilbur Chapman, but those trips had been few and far between compared to his new schedule as an independent evangelist. During that first decade the new father traveled year-round, staying in some towns as long as four and five weeks. He usually went directly from one revival to another, and he often made one-night appearances in other towns along the way.

He missed the children immensely. A continual stream of letters home revealed a man who loved his little ones, missed them sorely, and longed to know how they were. His pain was exacerbated in June, 1901, when Nell gave birth to their third child, William Ashley Jr. Billy was preaching in Harlan, Iowa, when Willie was born, and he did not get home to see his baby for another ten days. It was almost as bad when their fourth child, Paul Thompson, arrived in 1907. Billy was able to be with Nell when delivery time came, but he was not able to stay long. Elijah P. Brown, a preacher friend of Billy's who began traveling with him part-time in 1907, remembered that "Paul was born at seven-thirty in the morning, and an hour later Mr. Sunday had to grab up his suitcase and make a dash for the railroad depot, without stopping to even form a speaking acquaintance with the boy."

Billy had to leave home that morning for meetings scheduled to begin that evening in Gibson City, Illinois, a town a hundred and twenty miles south of their home in Chicago. The evidence suggests that Sunday was scheduled to begin preaching at Gibson City earlier in the week, but he either postponed the meetings for a few days or had either Fred Siebert or Elijah Brown fill the pulpit for him until the baby was born. Being home for Paul's birth was important to Billy and no doubt to Nell, because trouble was expected with this pregnancy and delivery. In fact, when she became pregnant with Paul her doctor warned of grave danger to her and the baby. The problems notwithstanding, she finally came through the nine months and delivery with a strong baby and with her own health intact but weakened. Despite the happy outcome, it had been a stressful and fearful time. It took circumstances as extraordinary as these to pull Billy away from his ministry to Nell's side.

Nevertheless, as painful as separation from the children was for Billy, being away from Nell was even more difficult. His letters home in the late 1890s in particular disclose a man who was extremely dependent on his wife for love, companionship, and daily encouragement. When she was not with him he grieved; when she was not there to help him with administrative decisions and problems he felt inadequate. In brief, he was not a whole person outside of her presence, and occasionally he put pressure on her to find ways to join him once they had a little more income after 1900.

We can get a sense of the extent of Billy Sunday's agony and insecurity over these long periods of separation from a letter he wrote to Nell in about 1897: "My own dear wife, and darling lamb," he began. "My how I wish I could take you with me." Then he wrote of a dream he had had the night before, in which he came home and found her in bed with another man. He was relieved when he awoke, he confessed, because he knew it could never really happen. He was able in the end to conclude on a positive note: "Well Ma the work here is greatly needed[.] I

82

really can't tell just how it will go[,] great crowds are coming[,] the men are pouring in[.] I look for great times here."

Nell was a strong person—much stronger than Billy. This is made clear by her letters to him before their marriage, back when he was depressed during their periods of separation during baseball season. Her strength was evident again in later years in the way she tended her children, managed finances, and bolstered Billy's lagging spirits through letters and occasional visits. Strong as she was, however, she was not made of iron. Indeed, by late 1907 she was breaking out in hives and suffering from nervous exhaustion—and she was finding it increasingly difficult to handle all the chores in their rented Chicago flat. Torn by the guilt of being at home when Billy would send her train fare and tell her he needed her, she was equally devastated when she went off and left her children under someone else's care. In fact, within a few months she was near collapse. Their daughter Helen was by this time in her late teens and off to DePauw University in Greencastle, Indiana, so she could not help at home. George provided no help either, for he was attending an out-of-town college preparatory school. With neither self-pity nor complaint, Nell shouldered all the responsibility for infant Paul and little Willie by herself. She also gladly allowed Billy to lean on her for administrative help in his ministry while she managed everything at home.

By December 1907, however, it was apparent that Nell could not handle the stress. Although she never complained or asked for help, Billy sensed her desperation. He got home nearly two weeks before Christmas and helped with the children and chores. He stood in the gap while she got some needed rest.

Billy Sunday was obviously a sensitive man. He loved Nell dearly and it depressed him to be a party to hurting her and wearing her out. In truth, he was as confused as she. He knew it was wrong for her to work so hard. But what were they to do? He sincerely felt called by God to do evangelistic preaching, and Nell unquestionably acknowledged this. They both believed that God was blessing the work and using Billy's messages to change lives and communities. Nell clearly wanted him to obey this calling, and she had staunchly and ardently encouraged and helped him from the start. The truth is that Nell was obedient and faithful to God as far as she understood his will. She served as a loyal and dutiful wife and an invaluable asset to the ministry.

But Nell was also a mother, and she wanted to be a good one. Was her place in the home? What was she to do if her children wanted her home and her husband needed her by his side? If Billy was simply being selfish and childish, she could put him in line as she had before their marriage. But the current problems were not so easily resolved. Billy was a deeply scarred man, and he could not easily do his work without her beside him at least part of the time. The expanding ministry was in dire need of an administrator. Billy had no one who could do that work as well as she could, and everyone knew it. If she could travel more, she could encourage Billy, free him to do the exhausting work of preparing for and delivering as many as four and five messages a day, and competently oversee the administrative tasks that he had neither the time nor the talent to handle himself. Furthermore, Nell saw that the ministry was on the brink of a dynamic new era, and she was passionately interested in being a part of it. She knew that at the very least she could help to shape the ministry and give it direction, and at most the question of her involvement might make or break its future.

All these factors notwithstanding, what about the children? Was it right to leave them? What was God's will? Billy and Nell were not certain. Consequently, Christmas 1907 was another time for prayer and agonizing decisions.

5 The Redemption of Urban America

1908-1920

"Oh, God, give me strength to do thy will in this mighty city."

A year before Billy Sunday's conversion, one of America's most popular novelists, William Dean Howells, published *The Rise of Silas Lapham*. The novel was a best-seller and, in time, an important source for historians trying to understand the Gilded Age. There is no evidence that either Billy or Nell ever read this book, but if they had, perhaps they would have made different choices after 1908. In Howells's novel, Silas Lapham, pushed by an ambitious wife, leaves his Vermont home and begins manufacturing paint in Boston. Mining lead from their New England land for use as the paint's base, Lapham begins to make a small fortune as a manufacturer. Throughout the novel the reader senses that Lapham's material rise is a dubious blessing. Indeed, it has the makings of a great moral decline. In the end Lapham faces a fork in the road. One way, based on opportunism and questionable integrity, leads to financial independence for life; the other path, based on absolute honesty, leads to financial ruin. Lapham chooses the latter road. It brings about an economic and social fall, but it is a moral triumph. By 1907 the Sundays faced their own fork in the road. As they prayed and talked, they also looked back over a dozen years of ministry since J. Wilbur Chapman informed them he was not returning to evangelistic work. During these twelve years Billy had never been without an opportunity to preach; statistics on attendance, converts, and rededications were impressive; and continuing reports of changed lives and thanks from local pastors and communities were reassuring. At the same time, the work was demanding and exhausting, living and traveling conditions were spartan, pay was marginal, and separation from family was painful. Nevertheless, the family held together, and even though Billy never asked for funds from the pulpit; there was always enough to pay the rent in Chicago and buy food and clothing for everyone. They even scraped up $875 by 1901 to buy J. Wilbur Chapman's furnished summer cottage for leisure time with the children at Winona Lake.

By 1907 the Sundays could have settled for a continuation of life and ministry as they were, or perhaps sought a few adjustments to make for more time together. Indeed, if they had decided that Nell would make the children and home her supreme responsibility while Billy took care of the ministry, the next thirteen years would have been markedly different. There is no way that he could have vaulted himself and his infant organization to national fame, material wealth, and numerical success without Nell's administrative skills. An inherently able woman who had picked up some of her father's business acumen, Nell was one of the few people in America who could have kept Billy calm and happy and at the same time reshaped his ministerial team into a nationally renowned phenomenon.

The choices they ultimately made late in 1907 brought fame, wealth, and impressive statistics, but they also brought a torrent of problems—spoiled children, tarnished reputations, massive insecurities, nervous disorders, and dishonor to the calling of evangelism and the cause of Christ. Before we consider the steps that led to changes in the Sundays' ministry and the good and bad effects they had, however, it will be instructive to see how the choices were made. How could two people, sincerely praying and seeking God's will, get so far off track?

First of all, it should be noted that while the Sundays were committed, prayerful Christians, they were not immune to the tide of the times. The period from 1908 to 1920 was a boom time in America. Farm prices were high, industrial production was up, and most Americans were earning more money than ever before. The buoyant optimism of the prewar progressive era was reflected in numerous reform movements engendered by prosperity rather than the sort of depression America had experienced in the 1890s. Material success was as easy to achieve as in any period of America's past. Fortunes were being made, and people who had been surviving on the edges of poverty were now climbing into the middle class. Hard work and self-reliance seemed to reward everyone who tried, including the millions of European immigrants who entered the United States each year until the war and the increasing numbers of people who were leaving the farms to make their way in the cities. Unprecedented economic opportunity existed even for blacks who were making the trek to the industrial Midwest and North from the tenant farms of the South.

If faith in America paid rich dividends to newcomers and natives alike, perhaps faith in God and service to his cause would bring similar returns. Billy and Nell were not alone in studying the Scriptures, pulling texts out of context, and then applying them to America in general and themselves in particular. They assumed that God's promises to bless his chosen people in Old Testament times materially and abundantly also applied to themselves and America in the early twentieth century. Billy was especially fond of Psalm 34—he sometimes wrote "Psalm 34" under his name when an admirer wanted his autograph. Verses 7-10, in particular, are significant in this regard:

The angel of the LORD encampeth round about them that fear him, and delivereth them.

O taste and see that the LORD is good: blessed is the man that trusteth in him.

O fear the LORD, ye his saints: for there is no want to them that fear him.

The young lions do lack, and suffer hunger: but they that seek the LORD shall not want any good thing.

Helmut Thielicke once noted in a sermon that "the worship of success is generally *the* form of idol worship which the devil cultivates most assiduously. Here is where even the most serious men have a weak spot." Thielicke certainly did not write this with Billy Sunday in mind, but the truth of the message applies. The Sundays came to believe that it was God's will to make his faithful servants successful—to ensure that they did "not want any good thing." Americans in this era counted as good things bigger houses, expensive clothes, one of those new vehicles called automobiles, and privilege and status as well. In short, the Sundays prayed for God's direction but allowed their culture to dictate the road.

By New Year's Day 1908 the decision was made. They would work together as much as possible, take the children along during summer and holidays, find help to care for the children during the school year, and build a sound organization to take the gospel message to larger cities. Once the pathway was chosen, tangible rewards were quickly forthcoming. And because Billy and Nell interpreted these material blessings as evidence of God's blessing on his servants, they pushed ahead with increased vigor and confidence. Beginning with a multi-week revival in Bloomington, Illinois, the pivotal year of 1908 ended with a crusade that lasted several weeks in Spokane, Washington. This latter meeting was the first time Sunday had preached on the west coast, a region with many midwestern transplants. It was his first venture in a metropolitan area with a population of more than 100,000. He also led five other big revivals during 1908. Much of the time was spent in Illinois and

Iowa, but a long stay in Sharon, Pennsylvania, got him further east than usual.

The successes of the year's campaigns served to open scheduling opportunities for major crusades from 1909 to 1911 in larger cities in Washington, Pennsylvania, Ohio, Kansas, Colorado, and elsewhere. Most of the stops during this period were in cities with populations from twenty to eighty thousand. As the crowds grew, newspaper coverage improved and the financial rewards were greater. Tabernacles were being built, expenses were being met, and love offerings were surpassing anything Billy had ever seen. From Ottumwa, Iowa, a growing industrial city of over 22,000, Sunday wrote home with unusual good cheer. The crowds were "overflow" and early on the $2,700 for expenses was raised. On the last night, five thousand people came to see him, and seventy-five came forward at the altar call. He jubilantly sent $1,000 home to Nell, sent his mother $50, and bought himself a Swiss-made gold pocket watch for $118.

The Spokane meetings were typical of the Sundays' successes by the end of the year. One young man wrote home to his Wheaton, Illinois, family that " 'Billy' Sunday is holding meetings in a large tabernacle here. Twice as many people as can get in wish to hear him. I do not suppose I can get time to attend any of his meetings." But he finally got to go because school teachers were "especially invited and reserved seats saved. When we got there however soon after 7 o'clock the tabernacle was almost full." He observed that "there are a thousand in the choir and the building seats about 8000 more. Several thousand are turned away every night. Mr. Sunday spoke on 'the Home.' "

Spokane was a mere prelude to what the next few years held. Billy would write home telling Nell that the opportunities to speak were legion, that "ministers and rich businessmen" were coming to him from other cities, asking him to come and speak. Both Billy and Nell were flattered at being sought out by the rich and high placed. Together they plotted schedules for two and three years in advance, eagerly accepting calls to larger cities, especially those in areas where prohibition laws were pending in forthcoming elections. Billy was hungry for opportunities to lash out at what he saw as one of Satan's greatest weapons against people—alcohol.

In any case, by 1909 Sunday was back in Colorado—Boulder—and from there he went to what turned out to be one of his last stops in Iowa (Cedar Rapids) for the rest of his career. Early 1910 took him to Youngstown, Ohio, an industrial city of nearly 80,000 people. During the next twelve months he crisscrossed the country, conducting crusades in Washington state, Pennsylvania, and Ohio. Spring 1911 took him to his largest city to date: Toledo, Ohio, with a population of almost 170,000. More Ohio cities were on the itinerary following Toledo, and after that the gospel according to Billy Sunday went to Erie, Pennsylvania; Wheeling, West Virginia; and out to Fargo, North Dakota. Next he preached in more Pennsylvania and Ohio cities, and he ended 1912 in Columbus, Ohio.

Billy and Nell were in Columbus for forty-nine days, carrying over into February 1913. This was one of their longest crusades, and it netted them their largest offering to date—almost $21,000. Averaging out to nearly $450 per day, this was an incredible wage for anyone in 1913, much less for an itinerant evangelist. Indeed, the Columbus revival brought the first serious questions about Sunday's motives, with a few commentators asking if money could be his inspiration rather than the Holy Spirit. Billy and Nell shrugged off this sort of criticism, however, convinced that preachers had as much a right to make a living as anyone else.

Columbus, a city of 181,000 people, was followed by still larger cities and bigger financial and statistical rewards. After stops in Wilkes Barre, Pennsylvania; South Bend, Indiana; Steubenville, Ohio; and Johnstown, Pennsylvania, the Sundays rolled into Pittsburgh, the first city where they ministered to a population of over half a million. Offerings at Wilkes Barre ($22,188), South Bend ($11,200), and Johnstown ($14,000) were good, but they did not approach the $46,000 raised during fifty-six days of preaching in Pittsburgh. It was not missed by some reporters that Sunday earned for himself—after expenses —$870 a day, not counting his Mondays off each week. To be sure, Billy usually spoke about four times a day, but that was still over $217 per sermon—no paltry stipend considering that the national average income per gainfully employed person in early 1914 was only $836 annually—$34 a year less than the $870 Billy Sunday pulled down per day in Pittsburgh.

As it turned out, Pittsburgh was just the beginning of several more years of bigger cities and larger offerings. Denver and Colorado Springs, with populations of 213,000 and 29,000, brought in only $10,000 and $5,600 respectively, but Philadelphia, with a population of 1,293,000, produced love offerings totaling $51,136.85. Baltimore (population 558,485) gave $40,000, and Boston (population 670,585) brought the giving up to $55,000. In 1917, New York City, a sprawling Sodom of almost five million, gave freewill love offerings to Sunday of over $120,500, and Chicago, a Gomorrah of over two million, gave $58,000 the following year. The Sundays donated all of the New York City offering to the war effort, and Chicago's love offering went to Pacific Garden Mission. Even so, in the thirteen years from 1908 to 1920, the Sundays earned over a million dollars—a fortune by anyone's standards during those years, when the average gainfully employed worker would have earned a total of less than $14,000 for the same period.

More than monetary contributions went up in the 1908-1920 era: attendance and converts—so-called "trail hitters"— increased as well. The term "trail hitters," or people who walked the "sawdust trail," went back to the Sundays' 1910 Bellingham, Washington, revival. In those days lumberjacks would enter a deep, dark forest to scale the timber or calculate how much could be cut from an area. Because it was virgin territory, there were no trails by which to enter and return. Rather than use a compass, the lumbermen carried bags of sawdust on their shoulders. As they entered the woods, they left a trail of sawdust so they could easily retrace their steps to their point of entry.

Mrs. Sunday said, "In that country, that sawdust trail represents coming from what would have been a lost condition to a saved condition—from a dark, uninteresting and unsatisfactory place to back home, to light, and comfort, and friends and family." She remembered that in Bellingham "Billy had been preaching for seven or eight nights . . . without giving an invitation, and finally he decided that it was time to give one. And, as people started to go forward and take Billy's hand to accept the Lord Jesus Christ as their Savior, some man spoke up aloud in the meeting and said, 'oh, they're hitting the sawdust trail.'" The analogy was appropriate because their walk represented a path from darkness to light. Furthermore, the dirt floors of all the tabernacles were covered with sawdust, which was used because it held down the dust, it could be swept out and replaced to keep the buildings clean and sweet-smelling, and it was less expensive and quieter than a wood floor.

As might be expected, the number of trail hitters dropped as a percentage of the total population as Billy began to visit cities with larger populations. Nevertheless, the absolute numbers of trail hitters skyrocketed during these twelve years. Hundreds of thousands went forward as the years went by. A sampling of the trail hitter totals is impressive:

City	Year	Trail Hitters
Philadelphia	1915	41,724
Syracuse	1915	21,155
Kansas City	1916	25,646
Detroit	1916	27,109
Boston	1917	64,484
Buffalo	1917	38,853
New York City	1917	98,269

This provides only a glimpse of his results, however. Sunday preached sixty-nine revivals in sixty-eight different cities from 1908-1920 (he went to Syracuse twice). During these meetings he made numerous side trips to outlying towns and cities. He likewise made countless stops between major engagements.

When the numbers of people who came forward at prisons, rescue missions, jails, hospitals, factories, local churches, and Chatauqua halls are added to the numbers of trail hitters at the multiweek crusades, the totals are staggering. Billy Sunday had preached to over 100 million people by the end of his career in 1935, most of them in the years from 1908 to 1920. He preached to more people than any evangelist before, and conservative estimates suggest that at least a million people—probably more —responded to his invitation to come forward, shake his hand, and pray.

There were still other evidences of success during this time for Billy Sunday—at least by worldly standards. Not only did he preach in most major American cities, but he was front-page news in those communities while he was there. From 1909 through 1920 he was, by the *New York Times*'s standards, part of "the news that is fit to print" every year except 1919, frequently every month, and sometimes every day. During his ten-week stay in New York, he warranted daily coverage, and he usually landed on the front page.

During these years the famous evangelist was also the subject of over sixty articles in major periodicals, among them *Collier's, Ladies Home Journal, Literary Digest, Outlook, Harper's,* and *Everybody's.* And in addition to showing up in these secular magazines, he of course made the pages of nearly every religious serial in America, including Roman Catholic, Jewish, and Unitarian publications, as well as those of mainline and fundamentalist Protestant denominations.

And his prominence earned Billy Sunday recognition among the political elite as well. The one-time orphan whose mother could not afford to keep him at home dined with big-city mayors, Presidents Theodore Roosevelt and Woodrow Wilson, and scores of congressmen, governors, and senators. Invited to offer an opening prayer for the United States House of Representatives in 1908, the Rev. Sunday also stumped the nation to sell war bonds at President Wilson's behest. As a result of this national service, he met and dined with cabinet members, federal jurists, and high-level officials. He turned down several attractive invitations to preach in Great Britain and speak to armed forces in Europe because the president persuaded him he could do more for the war effort if he stayed home.

Sunday also sat in the drawing rooms of the economic and social elite. John D. Rockefeller, Jr., became a special friend. He invited Billy to New York, saw that funds were guaranteed to cover crusade expenses, and had both of the Sundays to dinner with him and his wife on several occasions. The correspondence between the two men was cordial and personal, and it is apparent that Rockefeller believed Sunday could reach the masses with the gospel of Jesus Christ in a way no one among the clerical elite would or could. Rockefeller was accused of using the evangelist for political purposes, but this is unfair. Billy was a life-long conservative Republican. His personal library and wall hangings show that he idolized such men as Abraham Lincoln, Ulysses S. Grant, Theodore Roosevelt, William H. Taft, Warren Harding, and Calvin Coolidge. Rockefeller did not have to buy Sunday's support for his economic and political programs: he already had it. The truth is that Rockefeller sincerely wanted to see the Christian message spread, and he felt that Sunday could take it to more Americans than anyone else. Furthermore, the lean and soft-spoken aristocrat loathed what alcohol was doing to Americans, and he applauded Sunday's efforts towards prohibition. To these ends Rockefeller gave Sunday weighty support, both personal and financial. He encouraged the Winona Lake warrior with letters and personal visits and contributed to his revivals, Bible conferences, and other Christian programs. Usually the only string attached was that the source of the gifts had to remain confidential.

Although the Sundays saw more of the Rockefellers than other members of America's social and economic elite, they did interact with plenty of others. Among those Billy ate or sat on platforms with were Elbert H. Gary, Louis F. Swift, J. Ogden Armour, H. J. Heinz, S. S. Kresge, John M. Studebaker, and Henry Leland. Sunday was also on speaking terms with John Wanamaker, George Perkins, and A. J. Drexel-Biddle. Some critics have viewed these relationships solely in terms of an economic interpretation of history, but this is simplistic. Some of these men were dedicated Christians who sincerely believed that everyone needed to hear and respond to the claims and promises of Jesus Christ. Others who had less Christian commitment nevertheless truly loved their communities and believed that Sunday would promote reform and improve the moral climate. That he usually affirmed their conservative political and economic biases was so much the better as far as they were concerned, but it was scarcely their only consideration in supporting him.

As Billy and Nell began to dine with presidents, judges, and tycoons, they also grew increasingly close to other celebrities. During and after the 1917 Los Angeles campaign, the Sundays were seen in company with Hollywood stars. They counted as one of the high points of their career a baseball game played in Los Angeles to raise funds for charity. Members of the Sunday evangelistic organization—permanent and local— fielded a team against show business personalities including Douglas Fairbanks. When Sunday's team lost to the stars, he jokingly said it was because they couldn't get a break from the pro-Hollywood umpires Mary Pickford and Charlie Chaplin.

As the Sunday family more frequently rubbed shoulders with the rich and influential, they began to display a taste for the trappings of wealth themselves. In 1911 they moved from the cottage they had purchased ten years earlier from J. Wilbur Chapman into a new home at Winona Lake which they had built at a cost of $3,800. While this abode was considerably more expensive than their previous house, it was not pretentious. In fact, the two-story bungalow with nine rooms and two spacious porches (it is still there and open to the public) was well-constructed and attractive. The house has hardwood floors and interior wood trim, but there is nothing extravagant about it. What attracted most attention was not this residence itself, but the fact that the Sundays also bought a ranch at Hood River, Oregon, at about the same time.

Other trappings of the good life enveloped the Sundays. New automobiles, among them elegant Buicks, Lelands, and Cadillacs, hurried the Sundays to many places in those years. Wherever they went they cut a stylish swath in their tailored clothing, fur coats, fine leather shoes, and expensive but tasteful jewelry. Both Nell and Billy dressed like pages out of fashion magazines, and photographs of the children indicate that they were outfitted in the latest styles, too. One picture shows son Billy in a raccoon coat and leather knee boots, and in a letter home in 1917 Billy instructed Ma to buy daughter Helen a coat of muskrat "trimmed with seal."

After 1910 whatever the Sundays bought required the mark of excellence. They even gave up owning ordinary pets. Billy's biographer noted that by 1914 one of Billy's favorite pastimes was sitting on the swing at their Winona Lake home, "fondling his valuable dog"—one of a fashionable (and expensive) breed known as the "king of the terriers"—an Airedale. The breed was something of a status symbol at that time. Other noted owners included Warren G. Harding, Calvin Coolidge, and even characters in the novels of F. Scott Fitzgerald and Sinclair Lewis. In keeping with their new image, the Sundays did not acquire the dog from just any breeder; they had him shipped by rail from a renowned kennel in Iowa. Billy was so proud of the animal that he mentioned him in sermons, and he was included in a picture of the family published in Elijah P. Brown's authorized biography, which went on sale in 1914.

Billy and Nell Sunday were certainly taking up with the economic, social, and political elite by the 1910s, but it is wrong to think that they turned their backs on the underclasses. Wherever they traveled, they stopped to talk with street people, and Billy invariably visited the prisons, jails, and rescue missions of every town where they preached a series of messages.

Even more remarkable, however, is the fact that Billy Sunday did more than almost any other white Christian leader of the time—either liberal or conservative—to reach out to

Afro-Americans and bridge the gulf between the races. A case in point was the autumn 1917 crusade in Atlanta, Georgia. While there for several weeks in November and December, Sunday made it clear to white leaders that he wanted to be involved with blacks as well as whites. Although he knew that to insist on integrated meetings could cause riots, he did hold meetings with Afro-American church leaders, and he spoke in several black churches. He also did several things no white evangelist had ever done in the South. First, he invited black ministers to all of the preaching services. Second, he set aside one night for blacks only. That night the 12,000-seat tabernacle was filled to capacity, and observers estimated that another 4,000 blacks stood in the aisles and around the building.

One black Atlantan stated that "Mr. Sunday was at his best. More than five hundred 'hit the trail.' This is unquestionably the greatest number of black people that ever gave their hands to a white man on a similar occasion." But even more striking was Billy Sunday's introductory remarks that night. With the white press there as well as the black, the evangelist said that Christ calls us to "cooperation between the races." He praised black leaders of history, and everyone in attendance said he did much to encourage racial harmony, which continued to be felt in the city the next day.

A few nights later, Sunday did even more in this vein, assembling an all-black choir of several hundred people to sing before a white congregation of over 12,000. A reporter for *Current Opinion* (March 1918) noted that

> it was a remarkable situation—an audience of Southern white people, a choir of Southern colored people and a Northern man standing between. "The very air," Dr. [H. H.] Proctor says, "was tense with excitement." The choir consisted of a thousand voices under the direction of a skilled leader. Picked voices from colleges. . . . Haunting melodies, the cry of the negro heart, resounded through the tabernacle. They were a revelation to the people of Atlanta.

The racial tensions were felt to have lessened the next day as blacks and whites mixed on the streets and in the cool places of Georgia's largest city. A leading black preacher maintained that Billy Sunday might have found the key to bringing the races together. "Just as David charmed Saul with his music and drove away his madness, even so the African may charm the Saxon with his songs and assuage racial asperities." In any case, several people thought it significant that the most popular song sung that night was "Goin' to Study War No More!"

The Sundays were doing what they could to promote racial harmony, but they were increasingly unable to identify with the poor people of either race. The truth is they were behaving more like the rich. For a season their lives were glamorous and almost ostentatious. No more sleeping fitfully all night in the chair cars of dusty trains. Billy now traveled first class in Pullman cars, and he insisted that Nell and the children do so as well. This was costly, to be sure, but the money was there. And now that they were well known and sought after— now that they could afford to pay for first-class accommodations—no one wanted them to pay. Most of the railroads gave the Sundays free passes good for a year at a time, and in nearly every city they went to after 1913 the automobile dealers furnished them and their staffs with handsome, new cars in the Packard and Cadillac class.

Meeting movie stars, business magnates, and politicians and traveling on luxurious Pullman cars—sometimes in their own private cars and compartments—were heady experiences, but the Sundays reveled in still more signs of success. In 1914 Billy made number eight on *American Magazine*'s "Greatest Man in America" list. His name or face also adorned the cover of several magazines and papers. His biography, entitled *The Real Billy Sunday*, which was written with Nell and Billy's authority and help by the Rev. Elijah P. Brown, became a top-selling book in 1914. Billy was excited when thousands bought his biography every night at revivals, and when even more bought the picture postcards of him and his family on sale at book tables in the rear of the tabernacles. Indeed, thousands of people stood in line in every city after 1914 to buy Billy's biography, autographed portraits of him and Nell, or any one of a variety of pictures of the Sundays together, separately, or with the children. Usually there were other postcards available for the souvenir hunter as well—black-and-white picture cards of the tabernacle with the name of the city and year and cards with pictures of the evangelistic team, in particular the musicians, were always on the tables for sale.

For the Sundays everything seemed to happen fast. Requests for both Billy and Nell to speak came in by the thousands. They were inundated with money received from offerings and through the mail. As early as 1911 Billy marveled when he learned that the Chautauqua circuit would pay him a minimum of $250 per talk and that he could pick up $5,000 in one three-week stint from July 25 to August 15 in 1912.

Along with the money and speaking requests came personal adulation. Everywhere people wanted to shake their hands, buy their pictures, and get their autographs. By the time of World War I a cult of personality had developed, and both Sundays were caught up in a swirl that was almost beyond their control. They could hardly help but enjoy the applause. They did their best to play their parts and encourage the flow, and they got a lot of help. The media—especially the newspapers—played Billy up long before he entered a town, and then gave blow-by-blow coverage for the duration of his stay. Reports of what had happened in the previous city were listed—complete with attendance figures and numbers of converts. Collection offering totals were announced, too, and then the inevitable questions were raised. "Can Billy Sunday attract larger crowds in Philadelphia than Pittsburgh?" "Will Sunday be able to crack Chicago?" "Which city will give the largest donations?"

In many ways the press put enormous pressure on Billy Sunday to perform. From about 1911 onward the papers were always implicitly asking, "Can you make it here? Can you top your own record?" Billy Sunday was a competitor and a fighter from his youth, and he instinctively took to this sort of bait. Nell enthusiastically joined in the fray too. From her Scottish-born father, who had emigrated to America and battled his way to success in his own business, she learned to take challenges as a normal way of life.

Feeding off one another, then, the press promoted Billy Sunday's campaigns while he and his wife did all they could to pile up numbers and dazzle the press. To this end Billy and Nell not only dressed well and posed carefully for pictures but they built an organization to see that the loftiest prospects were realized. Beginning in 1908, Nell traveled with Billy as much as possible, leaving the household chores and the children in the hands of a Winona Lake woman who came in part-time. In 1910 they hired Nora, a live-in nanny, who eventually became a beloved member of the family. After 1910 Nora did as much as anyone to raise Willie and Paul while Nell traveled with her husband a large part of the time.

Whether Mrs. Sunday was on the road or at her desk in Winona Lake, everyone knew she was the chief administrator of Billy Sunday's evangelistic enterprises. She screened the mail, deciding which letters should be answered personally by her, Billy, or a member of the staff. She also planned the revivals for two or three years in advance and made most of the decisions about where Billy could speak along the way and between major crusades. Three people besides Billy assisted Nell when she first took over the administration of the ministry: musician Fred Fischer and assistant evangelists Fred Siebert and Elijah P. Brown. But under Mrs. Sunday's direction, assignments were rearranged and a larger and more efficient staff was put in place. Grace Sax and Fran Miller joined the team to do Bible teaching, because Ma decided that they should hold morning Bible classes for women during the weekdays in most towns. Elijah P. Brown was reassigned to literary evangelism, producing the Billy Sunday biography and writing articles and tracts. Billy and Ma both took on writing projects themselves, depending on Brown and other writers for occasional help. For example, Billy Sunday's

Love Stories of the Bible was published by G. P. Putnam's Sons in 1917. Although Billy had most of the ideas and insights for applying the lives of such couples as Adam and Eve, Abraham and Sarah, and David and Bathsheba to twentieth-century life, the actual writing had to be done by someone who possessed the skill and time. And while Nell could write much more effectively and easily than her husband, she too needed some help for a syndicated newspaper column, " 'Ma' Sunday Speaks," which had a brief life during World War I.

Under Mrs. Sunday's direction the evangelistic organization acquired some key personnel that, in effect, transformed the tabernacles into entertainment establishments as well as preaching halls. Homer Rodeheaver joined the team as song leader and music director in 1909 and stayed for almost twenty years. "Rodey," as everyone called him, wrote music, played trombone solos, sang hymns, and directed the choirs. In the larger cities he located choir directors and made certain that choruses were in place. He treated audiences to gala musicals. The tabernacles in the smaller cities were constructed to hold five to six thousand people, with a platform for a thousand-voice choir. In the larger cities, such as Philadelphia, the tabernacles seated twenty thousand, and choirs of up to two thousand were accommodated on a platform near the speaker's platform. In the large cities there was music for an hour before Billy preached. This entertained those already seated while thousands more found their places. The music, too, was seen as crucial preparation— first quieting souls and then stirring them for the message.

Rodeheaver, a strongly built man at five feet ten, looked striking with his heavy dark hair and black bushy eyebrows. He did herculean tasks for the revivals, and everyone agreed that he was an important element during the years of fame and expansion. In Philadelphia, to cite one example, he found a chorus director named H. C. Lincoln, who, as Rodey put it, was a "veteran master organizer" who brought together five thousand voices from local churches. "We divided them into three groups," Rodeheaver remembered, "No. 1, No. 2, and a male chorus, each of about two thousand." To keep everyone fresh and free from back-to-back nightly commitments, "No. 1 chorus sang on Tuesday, No. 2 on Wednesday, and the male chorus on Thursday night. No. 1 chorus came again on Friday, and No. 2 on Saturday. Then they alternated Sunday morning and Sunday night, and usually the male chorus sang on Sunday afternoons, because we always had three meetings on Sunday, and the Sunday afternoon meetings were usually for men only." Rodey said that "because of the large number of churches co-operating it was never difficult to keep our chorus platform filled with good singers."

Rodeheaver provided more than just good choirs to inspire the guests: he played trombone solos and kept the people in high spirits and laughter as he talked between numbers. He frequently sang solos, and he also sang duets with Virginia Asher, who joined the team in 1911. The twosome was extremely popular, and they were accompanied at the piano by Bob Mathews or Florence Kinney. In 1912 they also brought on a little boy vocalist named Everett Mitchell, who, over a period of three years, brought thousands to tears as he sang such solos as "Softly and Tenderly Jesus Is Calling," "Face to Face," and "Where Is My Wandering Boy Tonight?" during the time of invitation. As an older man, Mitchell remembered that often, as he sang the invitation hymns, Billy would pace up and down the platform saying in tones audible to the first row or two, "Sing it, Son. Sing it with all your heart."

Along with Rodeheaver and the other members of the music cast, the enormously talented Virginia Asher did much to enhance Sunday's ministry. Born Virginia Heley in Chicago in 1869, Mrs. Asher was seven years younger than Billy. She was baptized a Roman Catholic, but her life was changed when, at the age of eleven, she heard R. A. Torrey and Dwight L. Moody. Later she did evangelistic work for the two men, eventually becoming a Bible teacher at the Moody Bible Institute. While she was there, she met William Asher, who was also a Bible teacher and evangelist.

The Ashers had only one child, who died at birth. This loss was tragic for them personally, but without the responsibility of a child to care for, they were able to devote themselves more completely to traveling ministries. From the late 1880s until 1911 they ministered on and off for Moody, Torrey, and J. Wilbur Chapman, doing evangelistic work in churches, jails, prisons, rescue missions, and nursing homes. Their ministry included tent meetings, songfests, and Bible studies. Both of the Ashers could speak effectively and teach well, but Mrs. Sunday was especially impressed by Virginia's abilities. First of all, Mrs. Asher made an attractive appearance on stage. Second, she was a superb singer; her melodious and strong voice made her a sought-after soloist, and after she joined the Sunday ministry she also became known for her compelling duets with Homer Rodeheaver. Third, she was a splendid administrator—something Mrs. Sunday recognized at the onset of their relationship.

The Asher-Sunday relationship began back in the 1890s. Both families were friends with the Chapmans, and like the Chapmans they all had cottages at Winona Lake. After many discussions about ministry, and from a neighbor's unique vantage point, the Sundays saw the enormous talent in this attractive and energetic couple. Then, in December 1911, Nell fell ill and was unable to meet her speaking obligations during their Canton, Ohio, revival. In desperation they asked Virginia if she would be willing to sacrifice her holidays and lend a hand at the crusade. Out of friendship she agreed. Before the multiweek services ended in early 1912, both of the Ashers had agreed to work with Billy and Nell Sunday on a permanent basis.

William Asher became the campaign advance man; he also conducted men's Bible studies and preached to smaller groups during the day. Virginia Asher was recruited to sing, speak, and lead women's Bible studies, but she was also asked to develop the whole area of women's ministry. Surviving papers reveal a remarkable woman with an incredibly diverse and thorough ministry. In advance of each crusade, she and William went to the city and got acquainted with businesspeople. Both Ashers had been urbanites since childhood. They knew cities, loved the people, and felt at home in cosmopolitan surroundings. Although Virginia organized women at every level of society, she was especially keen on reaching out to working women. Experience taught her that women who worked outside the home were most apt to be hurting, because the business world was where they encountered the most temptations. She focused her attacks on extramarital sex, drinking, drugs, abortions, and materialism generally. She organized businesswomen's luncheons and special services for women where either she or Mrs. Sunday spoke. At nearly every city revival there was one special meeting where Billy Sunday himself addressed an audience of women only, and this was arranged well in advance by Virginia Asher.

This able administrator ultimately developed the Virginia Asher Councils. These were permanent organizations designed to do regular follow-up work with women after the crusades. Besides establishing periodic Bible study meetings where women were encouraged to continue to follow the teaching of Christ, the councils sponsored rallies each summer at the Winona Lake Bible Conference facility.

Mrs. Sunday was the chief executive officer who oversaw Mrs. Asher's work and Homer Rodeheaver's musical ministry. She also arranged advance teams to work with men, and she orchestrated the formation of Billy Sunday Clubs—similar to the Virginia Asher Councils—designed to do follow-up work with men.

Running these big-city revivals also required advance work with the local clergy. Mrs. Sunday often went to the cities months in advance. She helped the pastors organize cottage prayer meetings, which were held weekly for at least a month ahead of the revival. In these small-group home prayer meetings scattered all over a city, petitions went up to God for revival, blessings, and guidance.

In addition to organizing businesspeople and pastors, there were also the tasks of finding a location for a tabernacle, arranging its plan and construction, and securing a guarantee of funds to pay all expenses in case collections were low. This work, too, was overseen by Mrs. Sunday, though she delegated much of the detail work to the ever-growing staff. In a few cities she did much of the advance work alone, without the help of Billy or anyone else, turning things over to her team of able managers only after she had everything planned and in motion. In preparation for the 1917 New York City revival, for example, she arrived several months in advance and found a suitable location for the tabernacle on Broadway at 168th Street. For Billy, herself, and the family, she located a house (Billy disliked hotels because of the crowds) to rent at 184th and North Avenue overlooking the Hudson River. She proceeded to work out the details for the tabernacle with various politicians and then met with John D. Rockefeller, Jr., and other members of the power elite who had invited the evangelist, organized the pastors, and guaranteed that funds would be available to pay expenses of the team, tabernacle construction, and extra police and fire protection.

Beyond this sort of organization, there were the endless details—as in all of the big-city crusades—of arranging and scheduling meetings, luncheons, and dinners. Meals had to be planned. A complex public and private transportation network had to be established. Someone had to see to the construction of a special platform and seating for the press, and news conferences had to be scheduled. Someone had to organize the army of volunteers who served as ushers and decision-card workers for the thousands of visitors at the New York tabernacle each day and night.

Billy Sunday did none of this preliminary planning, but he was aware that it was a gigantic undertaking. In fact he was so overwhelmed by how many lives were interwoven that it always left him awestruck. Sometimes he was nearly oppressed by all of the people and machinery. And certainly the advance publicity weighed him down and produced a powerful case of stage fright. There was no doubt about it: he was on parade.

105

Much time and effort was poured into setting the stage for his show. He knew he was expected to perform—and he knew he must do it well.

Going to New York City for his ten-week crusade was probably the most emotional and expectant trip he made since he went to Garner, Iowa, twenty-one years before. The only other thing to compare it to was his trip to Chicago in 1883, when he went to try out for the White Stockings. As the Sundays' private Pullman car pulled into Manhattan in April 1917, a wide-eyed Billy Sunday looked out on an estimated five thousand fans cheering for him and waving American flags. A reporter noted that he grew tense as they approached the city. Tears came into his eyes. He prayed unashamedly and loudly despite the presence of reporters and members of his staff: "Oh, God, give me strength to do thy will in this mighty city. Give me grace and inspiration to save men.—Help me."

Billy Sunday had reached the big time. The poor boy from rural Iowa had fulfilled the American dream. The world's greatest city welcomed him with open arms, its people identifying with his rags-to-riches pilgrimage. While the crowds cheered him on and wished him well, even in his moment of triumph Billy felt lonely and frightened. Only those in politics and show business who shared a place at the top understood his anxiety. The responsibility to perform rested squarely on the baseball evangelist.

The daunting job of preparing the way for Billy was well in hand. Mrs. Sunday had risen superbly to the task. She was now supervising a staff of twenty-six people—twenty-four more than she had when she took the helm in 1908—and together they set in motion the largest evangelistic crusade the world had ever seen. Mrs. Sunday summed it up well when they arrived in New York City in April, 1917:

> You know, we have thought of coming [to New York] many times before this, but I never would consent until I was sure everything would be done properly. It wasn't

enough to have a committee of one hundred [the original sponsors]. It wasn't enough to have the influential men in New York give us their money or even their sympathy. They had to be willing to work. I knew what it meant to tackle New York. Mr. Sunday didn't. He is always so wrapped up in the campaign of the moment that he can't make any plans for the future. I'm the one that has to look ahead.

Look ahead she did, and she did it well. From a purely statistical point of view, the New York City campaign was their greatest achievement. In a metropolis of more than 4,700,000 people, they conducted meetings for over ten weeks. Billy spoke to more people than can be accurately estimated because in addition to the regular services he went to churches, prisons, factories, rescue missions, and countless other places speaking during lunch breaks and his free day, Monday—speaking to thousands of people who could not get to the tabernacle. Other members of the team spoke too. We cannot know how many lives were changed, but at the formal afternoon and evening tabernacle meetings alone over 98,000 hit the sawdust trail.

Outwardly it appeared that God had blessed the Sundays and all was right with the world. But numbers paraded by the press told only part of the story. To the superficial observer everything looked successful and glamorous. Rumblings underneath, however, suggested tensions and deep, complicated problems. Nell had suffered in previous campaigns from hives and stomach pains, but midway through the New York meeting she landed in the hospital with more serious problems. She needed rest (she was exhausted) and surgery (ulcers and a hysterectomy). In the midst of this, Billy and Nell must have wondered whether it could really be God's will that they should be so busy and pressured that Nell's health was being destroyed. Was it right for Billy to be so busy that he could not be with her during her period of hospitalization? If they pondered such questions, no record has survived. On the contrary, the evidence suggests that they worked so furiously and traveled so incessantly that they avoided contemplation of any sort. They appear to have seen themselves as warriors fighting the good fight. From the daily news of war-torn Europe they knew only too well that many soldiers on the front lines had become casualties. Doubtless they felt that, like America's Expeditionary Forces in France, their task was to go on fighting in the face of adversity.

As long as the Sundays searched for measurable signs of success as evidence of God's will, they were relatively content. After the New York campaign, for example, they were encouraged. Invitations from other cities to do revivals continued to pour in—scores more than could be accepted. What they did agree to for the next forty-two months carried them to multiweek crusades in eighteen cities in twelve different states. On the list were major campaigns in Los Angeles in 1917 and Washington, D.C., and Chicago in 1918. During the three years after the celebrated New York crusade, the Sundays made their first swing into the deep South, with revivals in Atlanta, Georgia (1917), Fort Worth, Texas (1918), Richmond and Norfolk, Virginia (1919 and 1920), and large meetings in Florida at St. Augustine, Tampa, and Jacksonville in 1919 and 1920.

Well-attended meetings were not the only evidences of success. Trail hitters continued to come forward by the hundreds and thousands, though some people questioned whether these were genuine converts, people who were making sincere rededication of their desire to live a more righteous and Christlike life, or merely hordes of people who wanted to shake famous Billy's hand. To be sure, he always said such things as "Come on down here and shake my hand and tell me you'll walk with Jesus beginning tonight." Still, if as little as five percent of the people who streamed forward between 1908 and 1920 were truly transformed, then Billy Sunday was reaching more people than any other preacher in America. And he was offering encouragement to thousands of believers, which he considered an important ministry itself.

But the questions remained about what the numbers of

people responding to the invitations really represented, and Billy was too insecure to be immune to the implied criticism. Indeed, he asked himself the same questions. Of course he could not know the hearts of the men and women who came forward, shook his hand, and allowed him to lead them in prayer. In the end, he found the confidence to keep going in the conviction that God had called him to preach regardless of the results. And he was encouraged by the personal testimonies that came to him wherever he traveled. People frequently came up to him and said "I was converted at your meeting in _____ city or town several years ago, and I've never been the same." Letters continually arrived at Winona Lake from people thanking Billy for leading them to Christ and thereby helping them to change their lives. Letters from men and women, young and old clogged the postal service in Winona Lake, conveying thank yous and testimonials and praising God and Billy Sunday that they were now off alcohol, that marriages had been salvaged, errant children had returned home, and loved ones had died in peace because of his preaching.

The impetus to go on with his itinerant work was strengthened by several other factors. First, Sunday gradually broadened his agenda after the turn of the century. In addition to pointing souls to Jesus Christ, he hoped to stop what he and millions of others considered the decline of American life. Many observers—especially conservative Christians—felt that America was losing its moral fiber, and nowhere more so than in the cities. America's cities boomed after the Civil War. In 1800 there were only six cities in America with over 8,000 people, representing 3.9 percent of the population. In 1860, 141 such cities existed, comprising 16.1 percent of the nation's total population. By 1890, 448 cities over 8,000 held 29.2 percent of the population, and by 1920 for the first time in American history over half of the population lived in urban areas.

This massive process of urbanization was fueled by the industrial revolution, and the people who helped make it possible streamed in from the farms of America. Indeed, Fred A.

Shannon in *The Farmer's Last Frontier* estimates that eighteen million people moved from rural areas to the cities between 1860 and 1900. Millions more moved during the next twenty years, including hundreds of thousands of blacks from the rural South. Added to this great internal migration was the arrival of millions of European immigrants. Ten million immigrants (mostly from northern and western Europe) flowed into America between 1860 and 1890; another fifteen million streamed in (mostly from southern and eastern Europe) between 1890 and 1914. Such prodigious population shifts turned old cities such as New York and Philadelphia into giant metropolises, and newer cities such as Spokane, Denver, Kansas City, and Tulsa mushroomed into regional urban centers in just a few years.

The urbanization of America brought profound change— some of it good, some of it unattractive, and all of it disconcerting. On the plus side, there were more jobs and better living standards for millions of people. America's cities offered economic opportunities on a scale unprecedented anywhere in the world, and with upward mobility came new political and social opportunities as well. On the other side of the ledger, crime soared in the crowded cities, slums mushroomed, literacy declined, and conflict and confusion erupted as diverse ethnic groups competed for jobs and housing. Alarms sounded among churches, academic institutions, and welfare agencies, warning that America was in trouble. Families were torn apart, divorce rates rose alarmingly, alcoholism was rampant, and church attendance was down.

In the wake of poverty, crime, housing shortages, inadequate urban services, political corruption, and a host of other problems related to the triad of rapid industrialization, immigration, and urbanization, there came a multifaceted reform movement. Though they never came together in purpose or focus, so many people and organizations called for reform between 1900 and the beginning of World War I that it became known as the Progressive Era. Every group had its own panacea, and few Americans agreed about which problems should be solved first. Nevertheless, at the national level, both Republicans and Democrats responded with "reform" platforms in the early twentieth century, and local politicians forged "progressive" or "reform" parties or coalitions as well. Some Americans called for more government to solve urban-industrial problems, others called for less. Some groups wanted immigration halted; others believed it should be regulated. And so the debates went on until war came and turned everyone's attention elsewhere for a few years.

Like most prewar Americans, Billy Sunday saw a troubled nation, and he, too, had his cure-alls to offer. Like many of those who still lived on farms or in rural communities, he had a vision of an "American Way" to live that was undergirded by rugged individualism, hard work, and Christianity. Sunday shared a heritage with the folks still on the farms, and with those millions who moved to the cities from the farms between the Civil War and World War I. Part of this common heritage, this body of shared tradition, is strikingly revealed in *A Hand Book of Iowa*. Published in 1892 by the Iowa State Columbia Commission, it was a guidebook to the plains state written by Iowans, paid for by the state, and sent all over the nation as promotional literature designed to attract settlers. The historical portion of this little book captures an attitude and a way of life—a set of traditions and assumptions—that Billy Sunday and millions like him still clung to:

> Devoted Christian men and women came in with the first immigration in the permanent settlement of the territory. Loyalty alike to their God, their Christian profession and the moral interests of the communities they were establishing, they soon invited the services of the ministers of religion, and in their humble circumstances generously planned and labored to secure this beautiful region to the Dominion of their Lord. They endured privations, worshipped in lowly cabins. . . .

Billy Sunday joined hundreds of thousands of Iowans and Americans like them all over the land in swelling with pride at this kind of literature. But the truth of the matter is that it no longer described the sorts of Americans who filled the teeming cities across America. Churches were not being built, and a smaller percentage of the population attended the churches that were there. Nor was urban America at all like the picture of a uniformly white and Protestant Iowa: the cities were home to increasing numbers of immigrant Jews, Roman Catholics, Eastern Orthodox, and others of various faiths or no faith at all who did not fit this mold of life—and who were not inclined to be molded to fit it.

But Sunday was not attuned to the growing pluralism of America. Like many who shared his experiences, he was convinced that America was troubled because she had turned from her Christian roots. American morality was in decline. Newcomers were building more saloons than churches, and people spent more time drinking than worshiping. Too many Americans, he felt, were content merely to coexist with non-Christians rather than convert them.

And so Billy gradually began to give more emphasis in his campaigns to the goal of redeeming America's cities from a host of evils. All people needed to give their lives to Christ—not only to avoid judgment and eternal punishment but also to be led into a more righteous life. This righteous life to which he called people included regular church attendance, sexual purity, abstinence from drugs and alcohol except for medicinal purposes, honesty, hard work, avoidance of tobacco, dancing, and gambling, and more time for Bible study and prayer. Sunday and his supporters were convinced that if this moral posture was embraced, more than souls would be saved: entire communities would be restored to what God intended them to be, to what they were like in the days before the Civil War.

Billy worked especially hard for the prohibition of alcohol. Although he did not emphasize personal temperance, saloon closings, legislation against the sale of alcohol, or, indeed, any other aspect of his social redemption agenda as much as he emphasized the importance of personal salvation through Jesus

Christ, after 1907 he did preach his famous "booze sermon," entitled "Get on the Water Wagon" (reprinted in the appendix of this book), at least once in every campaign city, and he frequently delivered it in the smaller towns in which he stopped between the major revivals. It is impossible to quantify his influence in prohibition legislation, but most observers agreed that he helped make nineteen states dry and that he turned the tide in some counties in states that had local options. He also campaigned hard for national prohibition. He and millions of others believed that he played no small role in the passage of the eighteenth amendment to the U.S. Constitution. Adopted by Congress in December 1918, the Prohibition Amendment was declared ratified in January 1919, and went into effect in January 1920.

For Billy Sunday this was heart-warming encouragement. He was totally confident that alcohol was a tool of Satan—that it was God's will that the saloons be closed. For years he had been in league with fundamentalist Christians, the Anti-Saloon League, and the Women's Christian Temperance Union in their drives to reform America. No victory except the salvation of souls was so dear to his heart.

Another great victory for Billy Sunday was America's role in World War I and the part he played in it. Although he did not take sides early in the war, once it was apparent where the U.S. would stand he began lambasting the Kaiser and all that Germany stood for. He especially enjoyed the days after President Wilson's war message on April 2, 1917. It was two days after Congress's formal declaration of war (April 6, 1917) that Billy arrived in New York City to begin his campaign, and he added another element to his invitations there: he called people to commit their lives to Christ, lead a more personally righteous life, "get on the water wagon," *and* throw their support behind the war effort. The prevalence of people of German extraction in the brewing and distilling industries tied two of his causes neatly together, and until the signing of the armistice agreement on November 11, 1918, Sunday exhorted

Americans to use their booze money for war bonds. He also urged young men to support their country by volunteering for the armed forces—a choice he said pleased God, who did not want them sacrificing their lives to the ravages of enemy alcohol served up in large quantities by the Kaiser Bill's friends in America.

At the time of America's declaration of war in April 1917 only 200,000 men were in uniform. By the end of the war, more than 4,000,000 American doughboys were outfitted for service. It is impossible to determine exactly how much Billy Sunday contributed to the war effort, but we do know that he gave the $120,500 love offering to the Red Cross and YMCA at the close of the New York crusade, and he untiringly spoke to sell bonds, rally support, and encourage military volunteers. He was greatly encouraged, too, when soldiers wrote him from abroad, thanking him for leading them to Christ. As a consequence of his preaching, many of them testified, they were not afraid to die and they had been able to help other fighting men find peace of mind.

By the end of 1920 the Sundays had much to praise God for. Nell had regained her vitality, and she was back on the trail with Billy. Together they had invaded America's largest and, in their view, most sin-laden cities. If they had not totally conquered and redeemed urban America, at least they had managed to close some saloons, change some lives, and challenge the onslaught of modernism. In addition, they could celebrate victory in war, general prosperity at home, and Republicans back in the White House. They could rejoice further that in the last thirteen years they had gone from sooty, drafty railroad chair cars to comfortable, luxurious Pullman cars. They no longer lived hand to mouth in a rented Chicago flat; they owned their own nine-room house in Indiana and an Oregon ranch to boot. In less than a decade and a half they soared from obscurity to national prominence, with their pictures on postcards, magazines, and books. In brief, Billy and Nell Sunday had become rich, famous, and sought after. They had realized the American dream. By the world's standards they should have been tremendously happy. But they were not.

The Sundays wore a facade of smiles, but beneath the veneer was a core of pain. To a considerable extent, they could trace both happiness and hurt back to their being in the limelight. Famous people are always scrutinized in public. This was all well and good for the Sundays when they donated the $58,000 Chicago love offering to Pacific Garden Mission and when they gave the $120,500 New York collection to the YMCA and the Red Cross, but on other occasions the interest of the investigative reporters in their finances was less pleasant. And after 1911, the Sundays were frequently questioned about money. How much do you earn? What do you do with your money? How much do you think God's servants should earn?

Once in a while the evangelist and his wife were misunderstood and wronged by the press. There was some question about their Winona Lake bungalow, for example. When Billy tried to set the record straight by providing evidence to show that he and Nell had purchased it for $3,800 in 1911, and then spent another $1,000 to decorate and furnish it, some reporters ignored the documents and continued to assert that they had spent anywhere from $15,000 to $45,000 for the property.

The Sundays also came in for criticism for the book and souvenir tables at the back of their tabernacles, from which they sold thousands of copies of E. P. Brown's *The Real Billy Sunday*, Homer Rodeheaver's songbooks, reprints of Billy's famous sermons, and photographs and postcards. Some hostile reporters contended that these items were being used to squeeze more money out of a gullible public. It is true that the Sundays owned rights to the biography, Billy's sermons, and all the photos and postcards; and Rodey held copyrights to hundreds of hymns in the hymnals he published under his own imprint, Hall-Mach Co., Winona Lake, Indiana. It is also fair to say that they made hefty profits from these publications. But it was their position that they were providing the souvenirs only because the public had clamored for them. No one was pressured to buy anything, and prices were maintained at low market rates.

In fairness to the critics, on the other hand, it is clear that the Sundays were hardly free from the love of money. They stood in sharp contrast to John Wesley, the great eighteenth-century British evangelist. He also sold pamphlets and booklets by the thousands, but he gave away virtually all of the profits from such sales to help the poor and further the work of missions and evangelism, while he himself remained dedicated to living the simple life. In more recent times, Chicago's Dwight L. Moody, who preached on both sides of the Atlantic, was renowned for his frugal lifestyle and indifference to money. In similar fashion, two well-known evangelists whom he mentored—Reuben A. Torrey and J. Wilbur Chapman—refused to ask crowds for money at all. Like their teacher, they lived modestly, and no one ever suggested that they personally profited from preaching the gospel.

In the early years of his ministry, from 1896 to 1908, Billy Sunday had followed the example of his mentor Chapman. Indeed, while Sunday was preaching in Iowa and Illinois, the press frequently remarked that he never asked for money. This amazed the reporters, and it certainly helped make Sunday more popular and credible. Once the Sundays hit the big time, however, their concern for money grew until it became an obsession. As they rolled into larger cities, built larger tabernacles, and had greater expenses with bigger staffs, Billy gradually injected the issue of money into all of his revivals. No doubt he felt pressure to meet the expenses; he knew that if gifts were not forthcoming, the community leaders would be left with the bills. But in the early years he had been more casual about this. If there were bills, it was not his problem. God would provide what was needed, and he refused to worry, let alone make it an issue to detract from the gospel.

By 1911 or 1912, though, he was worried about money. Specifically, he was concerned that if he did not attract enough funds to pay expenses, the word would get out and it would hurt his chances of being invited to other cities. It is also obvious that once Billy and Nell got a taste of the good life, they craved more. To some extent they were obsessive about money. Mrs. Sunday suspected that people did not count the offerings correctly. She was also increasingly convinced that local expenses were not as high as people said. She kept a close eye on the money counters, demanded detailed accounts of expenses, and made sure that every penny in excess of expenses went to Billy and his team. Nell's obsession spread to Billy, who went from mentioning money just before the offering to bringing it up in sermons. He also was known to criticize the audiences for their stinginess on occasion. More than once he said, "Don't let me hear any coins fall into those buckets; I want to hear the rustle of paper."

This focus on money might have been amusing to some people, but even to Billy's staff and friends it became worrisome. Homer Rodeheaver attempted to criticize him for it once or twice, but Mrs. Sunday intervened, saying that such criticism would only "hurt daddy's preaching."

That money was perverting the Sundays' character can be seen in several ways. First, they were spending extravagantly on clothes for themselves and their children, and they traveled first class during much of this time after 1910. Second, although they gave away love offerings to worthy causes, and Billy often was a soft touch for old acquaintances who were down on their luck, in truth the Sundays hardly gave the widow's mite. Even as they challenged others to live by faith and pointed to Christ's teachings that disciples should not store up treasures on earth, the Sundays were socking away investments by the tens of thousands each year between 1908 and 1920. Their own records show that they held sizable sums in savings, and they invested thousands upon thousands in second deeds of trust through several banks in Chicago and other parts of the Midwest.

At times Billy seemed to agonize about their concern for money. Once or twice he wrote to Nell and said too much was being made of money. On one occasion she wrote to their son

George, who asked her to join him in a land investment scheme, and said in essence that she wished they could but Billy disliked having too many investments, for it violated Christ's warning that you cannot pursue God and money.

Clearly money was a problem for the Sundays. The more they earned the more it plagued them. The more they invested, the more they argued about it. Once they succumbed to gathering it in, there was seldom enough. And increasingly the secular press charged Sunday with selling the gospel. The religious press often reacted even more caustically. As early as 1914, D. M. Farson, editor of a Christian periodical called *The Burning Bush*, noted with alarm and sadness that Johnstown, Pennsylvania, had given Billy Sunday a $15,000 love offering. "The idea of a poor salary and hardship for Jesus' sake must be forgotten, if a man can become rich, as the result of evangelistic effort," wrote Farson. "If this is not making merchandise of souls, what is?" Three years later, when Sunday's earnings had grown vastly higher, another Christian periodical did a full-page spread listing all of his income between 1914 and 1917. In three years alone the total was over $600,000. "The ever-fragrant words" of Jesus Christ, noted the author, that "foxes have holes, the birds of the air have nests, but the Son of Man hath nowhere to lay his head, are in vivid contrast with the opulence, popularity and power of Sunday." The editor went on to note that "Sunday has made a millionaire of himself in the service of Jesus, and his trombone partner in the evangelistic team, Rodeheaver, is also a near millionaire, grown rich on hymn book profits," selling over 50,000 in Philadelphia alone.

These types of critics were legion, and they left Sunday at once angry, guilt-ridden, and anxious. But none of this criticism hurt him as much as that which he received from his own denomination in 1918. When the general governing body of the Presbyterian Church met that year, delegates were rightly concerned about the scandal surrounding Billy's income. They saw the dark cloud of Billy's greed casting a shadow over the entire denomination. Although they finally took no formal action, they did consider setting a limit on the income any Presbyterian evangelist could earn in one year.

Damage from greed was felt in other places as well. B. D. Ackley left the staff in 1917 after arguing with Billy about money. The ghost author of Billy's *Love Stories of the Bible* had to threaten to sue the Sundays in order to receive his pay in 1918; in the end they reached an out-of-court settlement. Likewise Billy's loyal associate, Elijah P. Brown, had to write several letters after he retired begging for the money he was promised for *The Real Billy Sunday* at a time when he was broke and the Sundays were so rich that Nell was placing investments in four midwestern properties.

The Sundays' money woes were compounded by serious problems with their children. Helen married in 1912, and while she was always frail and frequently ill, she was happily housekeeping in Sturgis, Michigan, married to a small-town newspaper editor and college sweetheart named Mark Haines. The Sundays helped them financially several times by letting them print the sermon pamphlets that were sold at campaigns, profits from which enabled them to buy a house and keep their newspaper alive.

George, the oldest son, was another story. He began traveling with his father as a team member in 1917, when he was twenty-five. Years earlier, when George was off to private school, he did not see much of his father, although Billy did write to him regularly. A 1908 note was typical. He told George something about the revival, informed him that the family was well, and then exhorted the sixteen-year-old to "Keep close to the Lord, George, and do right." But George did not do right. He emulated his father's love of money if not his love of preaching. He bought expensive clothes and cars and generally enjoyed the high life. Married several times to women whom Billy and Nell considered cheap and loose, he drank heavily, speculated in real estate, and generally embarrassed and grieved his parents. Indeed, in 1917, while Billy was working with George in the New York campaign, he wrote home to Nell with a heavy heart, explaining that his son had contracted a venereal disease.

Paul, who grew from infancy to twelve years of age during these years, missed his parents but was not much of a problem at home with Nora. During the summers he sometimes traveled the revival circuit with the family, and he was generally decent and manageable. Willie, who grew from seven to nineteen during this period, was eventually a cause of grief and embarrassment like George. A letter that Edward Fischer, a teacher at Winona Academy, sent home to his mother in March 1911 gives a glimpse of Paul, Willie, and their parents at this time:

> I have incurred the displeasure of the Sunday family and especially that of Billy Sunday, Jr., by chastising that member of the tribe. Mr. Sunday is building himself a bungalow here and Mrs. Sunday and the two little boys are living in the hotel part of this building. The littlest boy is a cute little fellow named Paul—3 years old—the next is Billy, Junior who is about 11 years old and awful fresh. He used to take a fiendish delight in running up when I was not looking and sticking his fist into that part of my body where I endeavor to digest my dinner. I told him if he didn't stop what I would do, but he seemed to think that I would have so much awe for his father that I would be afraid to touch him and kept on doing it, and I did. He hollered pretty well and said he'd be good. I warned him what would happen if he didn't keep his word and he didn't keep it, but I kept mine. He wanted to annihilate me then but I saved my life by picking him up and taking him to his mother. She is recovering from the shock, but Billy doesn't seem to have done so yet, and I hope he won't.

It would appear that the Sundays felt guilty for leaving their children to the care of others so often, and they may have tried to compensate by indulging their every whim. And other people fawned over the children and catered to their every wish as a way to please the famous parents. So it is not surprising that the children became enslaved to their own selfishness and exhibited the sort of behavior typical of this sort of bondage.

Out of four children, all of them were problem makers and misfits except Helen. There would seem to be two principal reasons why she escaped the alcoholism, self-centeredness, and wretchedness that befell the three boys. First, she was the oldest, and her parents spent more time with her during the early years before Billy was so famous. Second, Helen was expected to help her mother tend to the needs of the boys. The Sunday family was typical for its era: the women did most of the work at home, and the boys, like their fathers, expected the women to wait on them.

The letters Helen wrote to her mother after she was away to college and then married give evidence of a mature young lady who was deeply devoted to her mother, father, and God. Her letters also show a motherly concern for each of her brothers. She craved her mother's attention so much that even after marriage she wrote for approval about going to a physician, but she also demonstrated stability, devotion to husband and child, and a strikingly selfless attitude toward life. In fact each time her parents sent money or helped the Haines family in some way, Helen revealed genuine surprise and gratitude.

The boys, on the other hand, seldom wrote home. When they did so, it was usually to apologize for ignoring their parents and then to ask for money. We can get some insights into their relationship with their parents from some correspondence between Billy and the headmaster of Lawrenceville School in New Jersey, which Willie was attending. In 1917, at the age of sixteen, Willie was midway through the second semester and failing in French. He persuaded his father to intervene with the headmaster and arrange for him to drop the foreign language. The headmaster wrote back to say that he would allow young "Billy" to drop French, take a lighter course load, and see if he could do better. He is a "good boy," the academician observed, but he refused to study and he disliked "steady routine." Getting frankly to the root of the problem, the headmaster emphasized

121

that the teenager was suffering from having "lacked supervision" in the past. "What he lacks most of all," wrote the headmaster, "is to learn to live a quiet life, and to form good habits of work." He went on to report that Willie had been asking for the Buick that Billy had promised him, but he was opposed to such a gift on the grounds that it would only provide "another distraction" from the work at hand.

The problems Billy and Nell had with their children and their money resulted from some serious lapses of good judgment. They continued to talk about doing "God's work" and wanting more than anything to be in "God's will," but such rhetoric notwithstanding, they had obviously strayed beyond scriptural guidelines for discipleship. That Billy had deluded himself is evident in a series of contradictions that he was probably too blind to see. In February 1917, Frank Spellman, president of the United States Circus Corporation, offered Billy $2,000 per day if he would preach inside his fairgrounds during the summer. When the *Chicago Tribune* got wind of the offer, they asked Sunday to respond to it publicly. He said he was grateful for the offer in the same way he had been grateful for opportunities to earn a fortune each summer on the Chautauqua circuit. "But I know my mission is to preach the Gospel . . . two and three times a day [and therefore when summer comes] I usually slip away to Hood River, Oregon, to a tent we have underneath the fir and pine trees and there eat and sleep and build up and gain strength to go after the Devil again as hard as I know how."

This somewhat self-righteous refusal to allow anything—even the opportunity to earn big money—to interfere with his God-sent call to preach was commendable and consistent with Sunday's proclamations since the early 1890s. Nevertheless, one wonders what eventually happened to his constant and confident reference to Isaiah 61:1, "The Spirit of the Lord God is upon me; because the Lord hath anointed me to preach . . . ," or what spirit he was listening to by late 1919 and early 1920, when he seemed to indicate that he was willing to give up preaching for politics.

By 1920 it was obvious that the nation was weary of Woodrow Wilson, Democrats, and the age of reform. It was all but certain that a Republican would be elected to the White House in 1920. All manner of Republican candidates sprang up in this sure-win environment, and the name of Billy Sunday was included among them. Some said that he was the sort of man who could redeem the nation as well as the cities where he had preached. When asked if he would consider accepting the Republican presidential nomination, Billy and Nell did not have to wrestle in prayer for days to seek God's will. Immediately the evangelist's response was that he supported his friend Gen. Leonard Wood for president, but if he were nominated by popular demand, he would accept. Indeed, he then proceeded to list his cabinet appointees. He would make his old buddy Wood secretary of war, Herbert Hoover postmaster general, and Chicago's Judge Kenesaw M. Landis attorney general. Regarding the post of secretary of state he had not made up his mind; it was a toss-up between Nell and Henry Cabot Lodge.

The Republican party thanked Billy for his willingness to serve and went on to nominate Ohio Senator Warren G. Harding, leaving the evangelist no place to serve except as a nominee for the vice presidential slot on the Prohibition Party. Harding went on to a solid victory in 1920, with Calvin Coolidge of Massachusetts as his vice president. Less than three years later, only Harding's shocking death prevented the collapse of his scandal-ridden administration.

Good Republicans that they were, the Sundays grieved over President Harding's passing. But not for long. They had their own scandals to worry about.

6 Agony and Decline

1921-1935

"I wonder what next the devil will frame upon me to try and break me down."

Billy Sunday was neither an intellectual nor an avid reader. Nevertheless, he had a personal library of about two hundred volumes, and the evidence suggests that he read his books rather than keeping them for show. A few books, like ones on Abraham Lincoln and U. S. Grant's *Memoirs*, reflect Sunday's genuine love of American history and the Republican party. But most of his library was built around his interests in evangelism and revival. Charles Finney's *Revival Lectures* and biographies of Dwight L. Moody—one by Moody's son and another by George T. Davis—were interspersed with such volumes as Gipsy Smith's *Autobiography* and R. A. Torrey's *Gospel for Today* and *Talks to Men*. Sunday's library held few Bible commentaries or works on theology; it was weighted much more toward works of a devotional nature, especially those by authors associated with England's Keswick conferences and the deeper-life movement. Sunday was very keen on books by F. B. Meyer and A. B. Simpson.

It seems no writer influenced Sunday more than E. M.

Bounds. *Preacher and Prayer* (entitled *Power through Prayer* in later editions) was Bounds's most popular book, and it almost certainly touched Sunday's life and influenced his approach to ministry. Indeed, everyone who knew the baseball evangelist observed that he was devoted to prayer. He was often overheard praying while riding about in cars or on trains, apparently oblivious to the presence of other people. On his way to speaking engagements he could be observed talking things over with God, exuding a confidence that the Lord was sitting there next to him.

As important as *Preacher and Prayer* seems to have been to Sunday, another of E. M. Bounds's works affected him even more—*Satan: His Personality, Power, and Overthrow,* which was published posthumously in 1922. Sunday's copy of this book survives, complete with the inscription "To my Eternal Friend, Rev. Wm. A. Sunday D.D. with Great Love and Admiration, J. G. Hubar, Dayton, Ohio, November 18, 1922." The book also contains Sunday's typical marginal jottings, blunt-pointed pencil markings denoting the paragraphs he deemed most important. Billy was particularly taken with two sections of this 157-page volume: "The Devil and His Methods" and "Our Defense against the Devil."

The prodigious effect of this work on Sunday's thinking and preaching is manifested clearly in his sermons, especially in one he delivered at Yale University's Chapel, the topic of which was Satan's warfare against the faithful. The impact of Bounds's *Satan* is also revealed in the way Sunday came to understand the reality of spiritual warfare. In brief, the famous preacher came to interpret a series of personal calamities in this context after he read the book in late 1922 or early 1923. According to Bounds, this world is a battleground between "the children of the world possessed by Satan, and the children of God possessed by God.... Who is in us? God. Who is in the children of the world? The devil. [But] greater is He that is in us than he that is in the world." However, if we are blind to the enemy's machinations, if we fail to put on the whole armor of God as prescribed by St.

Paul in his epistle to the Ephesians, we will become immobilized during trying times. In Bounds's words, "the devil often tries to break the soul down and reduce it to despair. He tells us to discourage us that we shall never succeed. The way is too hard and narrow and the burden too heavy."

It was precisely this temptation of discouragement that came to Billy and Nell starting in 1921. The first of a long series of problems beset them beginning in January of that year. Soon after New Year's their son George walked out on his wife Henrietta. He had taken up with another woman. In the wake of this infidelity came several letters to Billy and Nell from George's destitute wife, begging for money to pay the rent and feed herself and their two little boys. When news of this scandal reached the newspapers, many eyebrows were raised at the irony of Billy Sunday preaching against sin while his own son was having an adulterous affair.

The second of a series of agonizing problems that hit the Sundays during the last fourteen years of Billy's ministry came during the Cincinnati revival held from March 6 to May 1, 1921. Family correspondence reveals that enemies of the evangelist in that city—perhaps they were part of the liquor interests who loathed him for his role in the coming of Prohibition, or maybe they were cynics who assumed the preacher was as corruptible as his errant son George—tried to entrap the Rev. Sunday with a woman. Because he never had an eye for anyone but Nell after he met her in the 1880s, he disappointed his would-be detractors.

Billy Jr. showed less restraint than Billy Sr., however. Word got out that he had gone to a speakeasy, consumed illegal drinks, and danced half the night away—despite his father's strong belief that dancing was of the devil. He was also discovered in a compromising situation with a woman companion, and he eventually landed in jail. Young Billy's behavior was the cause of even more embarrassment for his father because he was by this time serving as a member of the evangelistic team, as a piano player.

Photographs of Billy Sunday, Sr., taken during the Cincinnati campaign show him to be unusually haggard. Lines in his face and dark pockets under his eyes made the beleaguered preacher look ten to fifteen years older than his fifty-nine years. The tired warrior wrote numerous letters home to Nell saying he was devastated by the snide and knowing looks of hotel staff members. "I wonder," he wrote on one occasion, "what next the devil will frame upon me to try and break me down."

Despite the scandals swirling about his sons, Billy Sunday carried on as usual with six multiweek revivals in 1921, traveling from Florida to West Virginia, west to Ohio, back to West Virginia, down to the Old Dominion State, out to Sioux City, Iowa, and then into Tulsa, Oklahoma. He also made a few one-night stops in communities along the way as he crisscrossed the eastern half of the nation.

During 1922 the Sunday revivals were carried throughout the South in a zigzagged pattern with lengthy engagements in South Carolina, West Virginia, Tennessee, and Virginia. Except for a spring campaign in Richmond, Indiana, the Sunday team stayed in the South all year until the closing meeting in November and December at Dayton, Ohio. It was in this last meeting that Sunday acquired Bounds's book on *Satan*. And if he was not already convinced of the evil one's determination to discourage him and derail his ministry, he was so persuaded within a few months. In 1923 Sunday was strongly assailed by reformers George Creel and Rabbi Stephen Wise. Creel, a journalist, frequently labeled Sunday a tool of the industrialists. Wise charged that the evangelist went into West Virginia that year to dismantle the coal strike, that he was a tool of the mine owners, and that it was men like John D. Rockefeller, Jr., who urged him to go there and diffuse the explosive labor organization.

Sunday felt slandered by these accusations, but such assaults were not new. Indeed, he was assailed for preaching in Colorado during the coal field strikes before America's entry into World War I. It is true that the evangelist maintained friendships with such men as Elbert H. Gary and John D. Rockefeller,

Jr., that he was identified with the conservative wing of the Republican party, and that he sympathized with the capitalists and industrialists. But whatever his sympathies in the matter, the fact was that he prepared his West Virginia schedule well in advance of the strike. Furthermore he had been preaching and making contacts in those mining districts for two years before the walkout. In any case Sunday held multiweek revivals during 1923 in Tennessee, South Carolina, and Kentucky as well as West Virginia, taking on only one crusade outside of the South, in little Niagara Falls, New York. Such a schedule was arranged years in advance, and it was not subject to the beck and call of businessmen.

The strain of family problems together with the increased opposition to his crusades from the liberal church and press caused Billy Sunday to lean more heavily on Nell than he had in the past. When on one occasion he so despaired of the pressure that he considered giving up preaching, she left their youngest child, Paul, with Nora their housekeeper and came to his side to rebuild his conviction to fight on.

Nell continued to manage the revival programs, but after New York in 1917 and Chicago in 1918, the cities they visited were much smaller and the advance preparations were considerably easier to work out. The permanent staff was cut to five or six. Nevertheless, the lighter revival duties after 1920 did not free Nell to spend more time at home. Billy needed her nearby more than ever to help him get through the revivals and the flood of criticism. Much of it came from journalists and social reformers, but the most stinging rebukes came from fellow clergy who assailed his "gutter language," his "barnyard education," and his "medieval theology" with its emphasis on judgment and hell.

Nell remained loyally at Billy's side until the next calamity beset the family. In spring of 1924 she was in a serious auto accident. She was not critically injured, but she did need several weeks to recuperate—and her injuries affected Billy almost as seriously. The strain of this crisis compounded the stress he was feeling on other fronts and precipitated a physical and emotional collapse. On this occasion he was hospitalized for just two days at the Mayo Clinic in Rochester, Minnesota, but he returned the following January complaining of numbness in parts of his body. His physician attributed it to a nervous disorder brought on by overwork.

The Sundays managed to do six revivals averaging over a month each in 1924, and they did the same in 1925. This grueling schedule brought on another barrage of physical problems. Billy had oral surgery in December of 1925, and then Nell was immobilized with ulcers the next spring. She had stomach surgery at the Mayo Clinic, and was not away even a full year before a relapse caused her to return for more ulcer surgery in April 1927.

By this time Billy was confident that their problems were of the devil's making. So he plucked up his courage, ordered Nell to stay home and rest, and hit the revival circuit alone. In 1927 and 1928 he did twelve more revivals. Then in 1929 he took on another five, averaging five to six weeks in duration at each small city. All this time while he traveled, preached his heart out, and drove his body near collapse, he lived with the constant pressure of family problems. Preaching several times a day, Billy also wrote daily letters to Nell to keep her encouraged. She needed all the support he could offer, because in the midst of her recuperation she was forced to wrangle with lawyers retained by the ex-wives of both George and Bill Jr. In each case lawyers for the jilted spouses threatened to sue and make public disclosures of the Sunday men's infidelities. For stipends ranging from $5,000 to $36,000, each plaintiff settled out of court, and the scandals were kept relatively quiet.

Throughout these painful legal battles in 1928 and 1929, Billy and Nell Sunday felt betrayed by their sons and blackmailed by their daughters-in-law. On top of this, their youngest son, Paul, traveled to Europe for a postgraduation jaunt and left bill collectors at home to harass his parents for debts he owed to fellow students and his college fraternity.

Then in the spring of 1930, one more heavy blow befell the

Sundays. Their beloved Nora, the housekeeper and nanny who had become as dear to them as any blood relative, died at Winona Lake. After she was buried in April, the sixty-seven-year-old evangelist finished a month-long crusade in Mount Holly, New Jersey, and then made some substantial changes in his schedule. Thereafter he did meetings of much shorter duration.

It was good that Billy Sunday decided to slow his pace after Nora's death in 1930, because the burdens of his boys' sinful lifestyles, abuse from critics, and his own and Nell's weakened health were to grow even heavier during the next few years. In October 1932 their lovely daughter Helen, only forty-two years old, and the mother of their first grandchild, Paul, died from pneumonia. This loss was especially difficult because she had been so close to her parents. Never a robust woman, Helen was plagued by various maladies that sound, by today's diagnoses, like multiple sclerosis. She increasingly suffered from numbness in her arms and legs, and she eventually lost full use of one side. Although she gradually lost physical strength, her letters show a joyful heart, a deep love for husband and son, and a devotion to parents. Nell and Billy lavished gifts on Helen and her husband, Mark, paying off their house in Sturgis, Michigan, furnishing it at a later date, buying clothes and dishes, and eventually paying off the loan on their local newspaper. After each gift, Mark and Helen wrote letters of thanks for the gratuities. They never seemed to expect anything, and their gratitude was always sincere and abundant. No doubt the thank you the Sundays most appreciated from Helen and Mark was the happy home that they kept. They were in love with one another, faithful to their marriage vows, and they were good parents. Respected members of their church and community, they never did anything to bring ill repute to the Sunday family name or the cause it stood for.

Heartbroken by their daughter's death, Nell and Bill were wounded yet further when Bill Jr. failed to attend the funeral. George and Paul made their appearances at the memorial service, but Bill refused to make the trip from his Venice, California, home. Later he wrote to apologize, defending his absence by saying that he wanted to remember Helen as she was.

After the funeral the Sundays continued to answer their mail, sending words of encouragement and advice to those who wrote. Billy continued to preach, but his revivals lasted at most a few days rather than the usual four to six weeks. Yet even this reduced schedule proved too much for him so soon after Helen's death. In February 1933 he collapsed while preaching in Des Moines and was taken back to the Mayo Clinic for tests and rest. Nell announced that an early diagnosis revealed a heart attack, but later tests threw that into question. In any case, he recuperated for three months at the home of Dr. Charles Mayo, with Nell as his attendant.

After ninety days of mandatory convalescence, the old warrior, now seventy years old, pulled on the armor as best he knew how and set out once again to battle sin and preach salvation through faith in Jesus Christ. No sooner did he begin to regain his stride than he was hit with one more stunning blow. Their son George, remarried by this time and living in San Francisco, was involved in a number of risky real estate schemes. Throughout the early 1930s he had tried to involve his parents in real estate speculations, but Billy had emphatically refused, arguing that Jesus had told him to preach and not pursue money. In any case, George speculated wildly in California properties. With the onset of the Great Depression, his ventures not only failed to materialize but left him penniless. At least once his mother went to California and rescued him from financial ruin. On several occasions she sent him thousands of dollars. In September 1933 his new wife Renee wrote to Mrs. Sunday, telling her not to worry. George had a meeting scheduled with several high rollers; soon everything would be much better for them. Evidently this much anticipated meeting did not go well. Soon after it was over he took his own life, leaving behind a destitute family and a pile of debts.

Years later Mrs. Sunday remembered that shortly after

George's death, Billy stood gazing out the window of their Winona Lake home. Watching the autumn leaves fall, and looking wistfully toward the lake, he turned to her with tear-filled eyes and said, "Ma, where did I go wrong? I thought we heard God's call to evangelism. But look at our boys. Where did I go wrong?" Like the Nell of old she walked over and told him to buck up. "You can't blame yourself. You did the best you knew how. You followed God's will as best you understood it. The boys have made their own choices. You can't put it on yourself this way."

And in truth, he probably had been doing the best he knew. To be sure, all the fame had poisoned him in the flush days. Money and the good life seem to have seduced everyone in the Sunday clan except Helen. The large campaign income, with no financial accountability to anyone, left the Sundays open to much criticism, and rightly so. There was something fundamentally immoral about asking people to make sacrificial monetary contributions at spiritual revival meetings and then walking away with a large part of the take for personal use. It was especially unpalatable when the evangelist and his wife already had money in several banks, owned their own home plus recreational property, and held the second deeds of trust on numerous farms.

But the heady successes of the years from 1910 to 1920 were not to last. After this period Billy Sunday's ministry by all measurable standards went into marked decline. Paradoxically and ironically, it was the best thing that could have happened to him and the lofty cause he stood for.

After 1921 the major American cities never brought Billy Sunday back for a revival. After his Cincinnati revival in 1921, he held crusades in only four cities with six-figure populations: Louisville, Portland, Nashville, and St. Louis. To be sure, he preached an occasional service in a large city church, but his days of multiweek revivals in large cities were over. Revivals after 1921 were typically held in small cities with five-figure populations such as Elmira, New York; Jackson, Mississippi;

Bangor, Maine; and Newport News, Virginia. He also made plenty of monthly stops in smaller towns such as Cape Girardeau, Missouri; Beckly, West Virginia; West Frankfurt, Illinois; Madisonville, Kentucky; Sterling, Colorado; and Dodge City, Kansas.

As the cities in which Billy preached declined in size and glamor, so did the final-night love offerings. Charlotte, North Carolina; Shreveport, Louisiana; and Memphis, Tennessee, each gave over $20,000 in 1924, but except for Winston-Salem in 1925, he never saw that much money from one city again. Collections plummeted to such figures as $8,400 at Monmouth, Illinois; $8,500 at Portland, Oregon; and $5,200 at Yakima, Washington. Eventually offerings went even lower. After paying off the lawyers who sued their sons, helping to support destitute grandchildren, and cleaning up George and Bill's debts, the Sundays found they had hardly anything but the Oregon and Winona Lake properties left. Nell and Billy wrote candidly to one another about the possibility of actually going broke.

More dwindled for the Sundays than their income, their savings, and the size of the cities where Billy preached. Smaller crowds greeted them, and fewer people hit the sawdust trail. Indeed, they seemed to be nearing a full-circle return to the kerosene circuit days. Crowds were respectable but not spectacular—numbering five or six hundred to maybe a thousand. Love offerings were generous but hardly remarkable, no reporters but those of the local press attended the services, and hotel accommodations were one or two star rather than four. Length of stay in these communities declined, too, with Billy seldom preaching more than a few nights in any one town. By the mid-1920s communities stopped building tabernacles, and the old baseball evangelist had to be satisfied with a packed church rather than overflow crowds in a building made to specifications with his name emblazoned on the outside.

For the most part, Billy's name was no longer seen in the pages of the *New York Times* unless one of his sons had gotten into more trouble. Preaching to several hundred people in Kentucky or Indiana was not newsworthy by the *Times*'s standards. Nor did reporters any longer ask Mr. Sunday if he was running for political office. And after the Coolidges left Washington, the Sundays made only one more visit to the White House—and that invitation came only after they wrote to President Hoover, said they would be in Washington, and asked if they could drop by to say hello.

Billy Sunday was convinced that these years of agony and decline were the results of Satan's attacks. His music director, Homer Rodeheaver, had a different interpretation. Rodey resigned after two decades with the famous evangelist because he was no longer comfortable with the leadership of the organization. His problems with Billy Sunday went back to the early 1920s. The Sundays had always said that they were open to the staff's suggestions for improvement, but when he had tried to talk to them about issues that disturbed the staff or things they could do to improve community relations and the overall ability to minister, he felt that they were unresponsive.

In July 1927, after several years of frustration and failure to communicate in person, Rodey put down his thoughts in a seven-page letter and sent it to Mrs. Sunday. He was full of thanks for all that the Sundays had done for him since he joined them in 1909, but he also took note of how he had tried to repay their kindnesses by working "hard and conscientiously. There has never been a single place where our choruses have not built up and increased in numbers and efficiency." Furthermore, he continued, "my work outside has been more strenuous than in the tabernacle. I have never shirked a single duty if I knew it." Having established his loyalty to their ministry, the popular vocalist proceeded to list several reasons why he thought it was in decline, and he offered positive steps for improvement.

First of all, Billy Sunday had grown increasingly nervous and irritable on the platform, and this was adversely affecting the musicians. This had been going on, Rodey noted, since before 1925. Sometimes Billy would walk up and down while he and Virginia Asher were singing a duet, and once in a while he would even step between them in the midst of a song in order to lay his Bible on the podium. When he wasn't pacing, he was fidgeting with his Bible, shifting nervously in his chair, looking irritated and impatient, and even letting out a loud sigh of chagrin. These antics distracted not only the soloists but the congregation as well, wrote Rodeheaver.

He noted that the musicians had even more complaints. Billy tended to forget that the music was part of the same fabric as the message. A lot of effort was put into selecting music that would touch people's hearts and prepare them for the theme of the sermon, and yet Billy often seemed to treat it as a bother, cut it short, or leave part of it out altogether. Rodeheaver acknowledged that Billy had a right to do away with the music as he wished, but he thought he should know that this attitude was causing a constant turnover in musicians—and was leading Rodeheaver to question his interest in the campaigns as well.

In hopes that Mrs. Sunday would be able to initiate some corrective changes, Rodeheaver wrote, he wanted to mention yet more problems, "things which his own friends have repeatedly mentioned to me," things that needed to be examined and corrected. "First of all, and I believe most important of all," was the change "in his method of giving the invitation. In the days when such tremendous results were following the invitations, no one could have any reason or right to make any criticism or suggestion. As the results have been diminishing," he continued, "there must be a reason." The reason, as Rodeheaver saw it, was this:

> Great men of the country used to be amazed at the tremendous power he had in getting men and women to publicly confess Christ. One very prominent man said to me one time, "It must be because of his holy boldness." That particular thing seems to have gone almost entirely out of his invitations and very rarely does he give a definite, clear invitation for people to forsake their sins and come and publicly accept Christ as their Saviour. We have not been in a meeting during the last 3 or 4 years where the ministers

have not come to me and asked if some suggestions could not be made to Mr. Sunday to make his invitation clear and plain.

In brief, Rodeheaver maintained that although Billy was preaching his sermons with the same power as before, he had begun to call people forward on a variety of pretexts but not for the specific purpose of repentance and faith in Christ as he had in the old days. "When he makes his proposition for everybody to come it loses its effect because people cannot see any definite, specific thing for which they should come." On occasion, he extended the invitation not to individuals but to whole clubs or organizations. Many refused to respond to these collective calls because "they did not want to suffer . . . misunderstanding and embarrassment." Rodeheaver also noted that Sunday's "argument that he has never given an invitation where no one has come" bothered many people attending the revivals because it "is not in itself a real reason for people to come to accept Christ."

Some people were also taking offense at Billy's behavior after he had made the invitation to come forward. After he comes down off the platform, Rodey said,

> the people begin to come and if there is the slightest bit of congestion, he shouts to the ushers and secretaries angrily and I have seen people reach up to get his hand and a sudden look of fear or astonishment come into their face because he was not looking at them but shouting something which they could not understand. Then, I have seen other serious men and women coming along in line with bowed heads, the most serious moment that they have in their lives, expecting a direct word and hearty hand clasp from the man who asked them to take this step, and when they got up there he would be looking away or talking to someone else and many times never look at the men or the women with whom he was shaking hands. I have seen them turn away with disappointment written on their faces sometimes refusing to go into the seats or give their names and go on back into the crowd or out of the tabernacle.

This devastating observation did not end Rodeheaver's litany of grievances. The issue of money, he wrote, was destroying Billy Sunday's effectiveness. He talked about money far too much. He had the executive committees on edge before they were asked to speak to the congregation. These men did their job well, he said, and they would get a good offering if only Billy would leave them alone. "I really believe he would fare better in his own offering if he would not go onto the platform until after the offering was taken. Many of his best friends . . . have expressed this, too." The music leader summed it up this way:

Sometimes Mr. Sunday seems to forget that when the crowds are small the collections necessarily must be increasingly small. He has bawled the people out here when in proportion to the number that have attended the meeting, they have been exceedingly generous and have given more in proportion than any place we have been in this year. If he would only consent to let the committees handle that part of it, giving any direction he may want to give off the platform and personally to the men, I really believe the men would be happier and the meetings more effective.

Rodeheaver had still more to get off his chest. He felt the sermons were too long. "When we first became associated, he had only 3 or 4 sermons that were an hour long. Now he only has 3 or 4 that do not go an hour or longer." He often preached an hour and fifteen minutes or an hour and a half. No one wants to listen that long, said Rodey, especially when he begins to speed up his message in such a way that listeners cannot fully understand his words.

Finally, Rodeheaver suggested that Billy was pushing himself and his staff too hard. He preached that God intends everyone to take a sabbath rest, but his staff was not allowed a day of rest after six days of work. He drives us for seven without a break, Rodey complained, and then we don't even get two weeks rest between meetings.

This letter, dated July 3, 1927, was not a notice of resignation; it was a sincere attempt to halt the decline of Billy Sunday's ministry. But when Mrs. Sunday read the letter, she told Rodey that she could not pass it on to Billy because the contents would only bother him and bring more problems to his tension-ridden life. Within a few months, having seen no effort to respond to his concerns, Rodeheaver decided that he could not bear it any longer. Without fanfare, and without making any of his reasons public, he slipped away from the Sunday organization and wished everyone well.

In 1929 Billy wrote a letter to Rodeheaver accusing him of ingratitude for all that had been done to make him famous and prosperous. Rodey wrote a firm but fair reply to his old partner saying that he always spoke highly of the Sundays and mentioned his gratitude for the opportunities they provided. Nevertheless, he urged attention to several complaints. Mr. Sunday solicited advice, but he never heeded it. Other preachers allowed soloists to select their accompanists, but Sunday would not. Other evangelists joined the team in believing that the music ministry "is a real vital and necessary thing," but Sunday never agreed. He told Sunday that his "constant driving and scolding about money from the beginning to the end of the meeting" devastated the workers. "It never comes to you but in every city we know splendid men and women who are alienated from you and your work because of the drastic, disagreeable things you say about money from the platform."

Rodeheaver explained that he had attempted to say these things to Billy for years, and he specifically mentioned the letter he had tried to get to him through Nell two years before. He reiterated his suggestion that he cut his sermons to forty-five or fifty minutes and he urged him to clarify and narrow his invitations. Finally, he pointed out a previously unmentioned reason why the Billy Sunday evangelistic ministry was in a slump. Rodeheaver obviously remembered the early years of the century when Billy always had time for the pastors of the churches in the cities and towns where he spoke. In essence he became a pastor to the pastors. He talked with them, encouraged them, and listened to their woes. But once he became a celebrity, he no longer had time for local pastors and townspeople—the people he used to eat chicken and play ball with. Although Sunday's old friend did not remind him of the old days, he did ask a thought-provoking question: "I wonder if you ever realize how much you miss by not being a little more friendly with some of the folks in every town who would like to be friendly with you." Finally, in a spirit of concern—of tough love rather than bitterness—he noted that the ministry was less effective because of low staff morale. And morale was down, he said, because Billy seldom had time to visit or have a meal with his own people— several of whom, by the way, were in dire need of more money.

Thus the handsome and self-assured Rodeheaver laid the cause of the ministry's decline at the evangelist's own door. It must have been difficult for Sunday to receive this criticism from his old colleague, and more difficult still to accept the truth of it. He was firmly convinced that at least some of his problems resulted from satanic opposition to his extraordinarily effective ministry, and he must have been tempted to assume that this was the source of all of his misery. But to his credit, Billy did take Rodeheaver's criticisms seriously. Indeed, he set about making some of the suggested changes, shortening his sermons and making his closing invitations more clear and precise. By 1931 Rodey was applauding his former boss for marked signs of improvement. After one sermon he happened to hear in December 1931, Rodeheaver wrote to Billy, "I appreciated the fine virile message. I appreciated also the fine direct invitation you gave."

The evidence shows that Billy made substantial progress toward overcoming his obsession with money as well. He not only stopped pressuring local committees and congregations for support, but he adamantly refused to avail himself of several lucrative offers at a time when he and Nell were feeling enormous drains on their resources. More than once Hollywood appealed to Sunday to let them put some of his messages on film. And those making the offers had an ally in Homer Rodeheaver, who worked to convince Billy that films were the wave of the future. After receiving emphatic rejections from the preacher on several occasions in 1930 and 1931, Rodeheaver, who by this time was a wealthy gospel music publisher, made a last-ditch plea just before Christmas 1931. Think of what films of your preaching could do to extend the base of your ministry, he said to Billy; you would be heard by people you could never reach personally. But Sunday had evidently learned his lesson. Neither the lure of rekindled fame nor the prospect of Rodeheaver's royalties could turn the aging warrior's head. He had tasted that fruit before and it was bitter.

During the last five or six years of his life, Sunday not only abandoned his former fund-raising tactics but also opted for a simpler lifestyle. He and Nell stopped spending so much money on clothes, for instance—though even so, Billy never became careless in his personal attire. Rodeheaver noted in his autobiography, *Twenty Years with Billy Sunday*, that to the end of his career "his suits were immaculate and were worn out more by the cleaner and presser than by use; certain neckties must be used with certain suits"; shoes were not so quickly replaced, but they received "new heels at the slightest sign of wear."

The reformed Billy Sunday also began to spend more time with local pastors and ordinary people. He continued to delight at rubbing shoulders with governors, senators, and presidents until his death, but he gave much more time during the 1930s to those people who lived outside the power structure. A cynic might say that as his popularity waned, he lost access to the rich and powerful, but that is only part of the story. Despite his decline from the pinnacles he reached in 1917 and 1918, Billy Sunday remained a famous American—a household name. The power elites in the smaller cities where he preached continued to want his time and attention, but increasingly he once again gave of himself to the middle and under classes. He frequently took time from his always demanding schedule to visit skid rows and jails, and in July of 1935 he altered his schedule so that he could go to a local rescue mission in Columbus, Ohio, for a reunion of all the alcoholics who had been converted as a result of his 1913 revival in that city.

Despite Billy Sunday's reformation and constant prayer for strength and protection in the face of spiritual attacks, there was no return of the success he had experienced before 1920. On the other hand, his popularity never sank so low that he was without unsolicited opportunities to preach. Indeed, not long before he died, ministers in California—including the prestigious pastor of Hollywood Presbyterian Church—tried to attract the septuagenarian evangelist to Los Angeles. Oswald Smith, the famous Canadian pastor and author, urged Mr. Sunday to do a revival series in Toronto, and several people in England asked him to bring his ministry to Great Britain.

Billy Sunday said No to all of these opportunities. The tide was rolling out on his life, and he knew it. Increasingly, illness forced him to cancel engagements. Sometimes he had to bow out in the middle of a week-long program. In a photograph taken in his garden at Winona Lake about 1933, he looks fit and trim for his age, but his face is sunken and drawn. Years of seven-day-a-week preaching—sometimes four or five times a day—had taken their toll, as had the burdens of fighting with critics, striving to meet increased expectations, and dealing with errant children.

By early 1935 it was apparent that the evangelist's end was near. Frequently weak and short of breath, Billy had a mild heart seizure that spring and was unable to attend the commencement ceremony at Bob Jones College in May, where he was to be awarded a doctor of divinity degree. It was granted in absentia.

Billy's doctor told him to stay out of the pulpit and do nothing more strenuous than putter in his Winona Lake garden and take short trips with Nell. But he was temperamentally unsuited to a sedentary life. He would not stand idle if people still roamed the world who had not been converted to the Christian faith. In Sunday's mind he had work to do as long as Christ's Great Commission stood—"Go ye therefore, and teach all nations, baptizing them in the name of the Father, and of the

Son, and of the Holy Ghost: Teaching them to observe all things whatsoever I have commanded you: and, lo, I am with you alway, even unto the end of the world" (Matt. 28:19-20).

The end on this earth came for Billy Sunday in autumn 1935. On October 24, a Thursday, Nell and Billy were gathering a few items for a trip to Chicago. They planned to visit friends and Nell's brother William Thompson, a Chicago florist. Just before they closed their suitcases there was a knock at the back door. Homer Rodeheaver had driven up from his lakeside house and parked in the alley. He wanted to know if the "Boss," as all of the old staff members called Mr. Sunday, could possibly preach at the First Methodist Church at Mishawaka, Indiana, the next night. Rodey was leading special services for the minister of this church. A crisis had developed that required Rodeheaver's attention in Washington, D.C., and he wondered if Sunday were strong enough to preach in his stead. Years later Mrs. Sunday told her friend Lee Thomas that Billy said "I'm feeling fine, Rodey. I'd like to go." She reminded her husband that the doctor said "you weren't able to take any more meetings." Billy pounded the table and growled "I guess I know how I feel." Her answer was "All right. If that's the way you want it, we'll go."

Mishawaka was a growing little industrial city near South Bend, about fifty miles from Winona Lake. On Friday evening the Sundays drove up to the city and parked in the lot of the large twenty-three-year-old stone church. The eleven-bell carillon announced the service, and because the word was out that Billy Sunday would preach, there was standing room only by the time the evangelist walked in. Nell remembered that "when we arrived, the aisles were packed and people sat even under the pianos and all over the platform. There wasn't room to step beside the pulpit where Billy stood."

There was no Saturday meeting scheduled, but Billy agreed to preach for them on Sunday night. "So we returned," Nell remembered. "It had rained Sunday afternoon and during all the time we were driving there, so the attendance was not as large as the Friday meeting." Billy Sunday's text was the question asked by the Philippian jailer, "What must I do to be saved?" According to Mrs. Sunday "It was a good Gospel message and Billy presented it well. He gave the invitation and forty-four people came forward. Billy was thrilled, and so was I."

That night, Sunday, October 27, 1935, was Billy's last sermon. The forty-four souls that went forward were the last to hit the famous sawdust trail at his invitation.

The next week the Sundays traveled to Chicago. On Wednesday, November 6, Billy and Nell were helping Will Thompson repot some plants in the greenhouse behind his home. Billy got tired and cold, and he went to bed for some rest. Nell took him a light supper of cold cereal and cream. As they had done on so many previous occasions, they shared one portion between them, and then chatted over a cup of tea. When Nell went downstairs to turn off the oven she heard him cry out, "Nell! Oh, come quick! I've got an awful pain!" He had severe chest pain, and it spread into both arms. The doctor came, gave him an ice pack for his chest, and went on to another call. For a while the pain subsided and the pulse grew stronger. An hour or so later Billy was resting well.

Nell sat by his side and answered some letters. In her little autobiography, *Ma Sunday Still Speaks*, she recalled, "I was answering one of those letters—I just got it started—it was to a man up in Montana. He was a Presbyterian Sunday School missionary way up there whom I had met and known. . . . Just then I heard Billy's voice." He said, "I'm getting dizzy, Ma!" Those were his last words. In a moment he gave "a great big, deep sigh, and he was gone!"

7 Legacy

"God blessed him so in his efforts while he was here."

In death as in life, the Rev. William A. Sunday continued to point the sinners in America's cities to reconciliation with God through faith in Jesus Christ. An estimated fifteen to twenty thousand people streamed past his open casket in Chicago's Moody Memorial Church on Saturday, November 9. For two hours before the afternoon funeral service a moist-eyed procession of visitors—rich and poor, black and white, young and old—streamed past to take one last look into the face of America's most popular evangelist. At least one man who peered down at the old warrior had been avoiding repentance from sins and a commitment to walk in obedience and fellowship with Christ. When he saw the dead preacher with the little New Testament between his lifeless hands, he cried out for forgiveness, and three times dedicated himself to follow and serve the Lord. After the funeral he was overheard uttering this plea as he opened the door of his car: "Lord, make me a soul winner." The rest of his life he used his printing trade for the production of gospel tracts.

The funeral service itself was designed to encourage the faithful in evangelistic work and bring those alienated from God

Legacy

into the fold. Many urban newspapers carried this Associated Press story:

> On Saturday they gave the Rev. William A. (Billy) Sunday the kind of funeral he wanted—a rousing revival service. They sang the glory song with zest, while the casket rested among flowers, and they pleaded with sinners to come down front and be saved.

Every one of Moody Church's 4,400 seats was filled for the late afternoon service, and hundreds of people filled every additional foot of open space in the building. Hundreds more, perhaps over a thousand, stood outside to pay their last respects. Dr. Harry Ironside, pastor of Moody Church, officiated. Mrs. Sunday briefly spoke, as did Homer Rodeheaver, singer Harry Clark, and a few others. The sermon was given by Dr. Timothy Stone, a professor at McCormick Seminary and former pastor of Fourth Presbyterian Church in Chicago. It was an evangelistic message. He urged those present who were not followers of Jesus Christ to repent while they had life. "Don't put off accepting Christ until the end of this funeral service," he warned. Many heeded his exhortation.

Several days later Nell traveled to Buffalo, New York, to speak at a memorial service for Billy. Reading from a little script entitled "Things I'm Thankful For," she spoke in a simple, warm way as if she were addressing a room full of relatives and close friends. "Folks," she began, "it's surprising how many things God can reveal to you to be thankful for, if you really want to know and ask him to help you. I had no idea there were so many." One item within the lengthy list of her blessings was this: "if Billy had to go, oh, how thankful I was to God Almighty that he called him in an instant." Not only was the evangelist spared the indignity of physical and mental deterioration that often befalls the elderly, but he was delivered from the pain of separation from Nell. "Billy Sunday had always hated to be separated from me—we were always together—and he would often say to me, 'Oh, mother, I wish Jesus would hurry up and

145

come, so we could go up together!'" In a manner that was remarkable for its selflessness, the recent widow announced, "I think God was so good to take Billy that way, and I thank him for it."

Among other items on her praise list was her pleasure that Billy never went without a call to preach, but most of all she said she was glad he "had plenty of people who wanted to hear about him, and wonderful friends he'd made in all this time, and so many people—God blessed him so in his efforts while he was here."

Of course not everyone agreed with Nell Sunday's confident assertion that God had mightily blessed the late preacher's efforts. Billy Sunday's detractors remembered his beleaguered family, and the taint of money followed the evangelist to his grave and beyond. Critics pointed to the pattern of dwindling attendance at the once-famous preacher's meetings, but others noted that, by any standards, Sunday's having preached to over one hundred million people in thirty-nine years, of which over one million responded to an invitation to make some sort of commitment to Jesus Christ, was impressive and historically unprecedented.

At the time of Billy Sunday's death, however, his style of evangelism was less appealing than it had been a generation before. Put bluntly, he and his style of ministry were no longer in fashion. When Sunday began preaching there were millions of Americans—eighteen million between 1860 and 1900 alone—streaming into the cities from farms and villages. One of these migrants himself, Billy knew their hopes and dreams, failures and sins, and he certainly knew how to communicate with them. When pastors who had been trained in prestigious seminaries accused him of using slang or crude language, they were actually criticizing him for speaking like those newcomers to the cities—the people he was trying to reach. His colorful illustrations and down-home vocabulary were tools that had proved effective in delivering his message to the people of small-town and rural America. As Homer Rodeheaver noted, "two dollar words" wouldn't cut it with Billy Sunday. "Every discourse abounded in epigrams. He used slang, but only such slang as was familiar to everyone in his audience. The accusation that he used the language of the gutter was not in any sense true." Rodeheaver had nothing but praise for Sunday's colloquial style. The evangelist "was a past master in employment of homely illustrations," he said. "Intimate scenes in the home, everyday experiences on the farm, the joys and sorrows of little children were potent pigments for his brush as he painted pictures of eternal verities."

It is important to remember that until the late 1920s and 1930s, neither radio nor the movies had yet attained the stature of mass media. Entertainment-starved communities turned out in large numbers to hear Billy Sunday if for no other reason than that his meetings offered something entertaining. According to a 1923 Louisville newspaper, "Sunday was a whirling dervish that pranced and cavorted and strode and bounded and pounded all over his platform and left them thrilled and bewildered as they have never been before." According to the reporter, he was simply "sensational."

From the few film clips of his meetings that survive, it is obvious that many of the spectators simply came to see a performance. One clip in particular shows a group of teenage boys grinning and joking around the platform as Sunday was getting ready to speak. In eager expectation they approvingly cheered his first words and gestures, much as they might have cheered the opening of a vaudeville act.

One newspaper editor said that "People had come to appraise Billy Sunday; they remained to praise God." They came partly out of curiosity about this remarkable man who had been born in a log cabin, raised in an orphanage, seasoned in professional baseball, and converted in a big-city rescue mission, but many of them left with more than just their curiosity satisfied. A reporter for one city paper sketched Sunday's impact and reception this way:

Sunday's pulpit phraseology pulverized tradition. Sometimes his speech was so plain as to be shocking—except nobody seemed shocked. His personality breathed from every word and gesture; and it spelled a noble purpose. The man has no new message. He embodies no modern discovery or cult or interpretation. He himself says he is an "old-fashioned preacher of the old-fashioned gospel," which is half true.

From the start Sunday knocked his audiences breathless with some of his expressions. He opened wide the throttle in each of his sermons and went the limit with his slang. Apparently he sought to unload his full store of picturesque and unconventional verbiage. There was almost a note of defiance or bravado in the way he said things supposed to startle or shock.

Most everyone was expecting a measure of Billy's slang, but nobody was fully expecting his smile. He has a smile worthy of analysis and description. It is a major part of the preacher's equipment. It takes the sting out of his biting phrases. For when he smiles the crowds smile with him—and that is often. That full-blown smile is the best interpretation of the man, for it shows his good will towards the world.

By the time each American home had a radio and every Main Street had a movie theater, there was keen competition for people's leisure time. Sabbath church attendance was not greatly affected by the rapid rise of the entertainment industry, but revivals conducted in big tents and tabernacles night after night for several weeks running were definitely undercut when the public found new competitors for their time.

But the decline in Billy Sunday's popularity was hastened by more than the public's easy access to movies and radio programs. A wave of secularism began to sweep the nation in the 1920s. For better or worse, national events such as the Scopes trial in July 1925, in which a Dayton, Tennessee, school instructor was convicted for teaching evolution as history, brought ill repute to the cause of conservative biblical Christianity.

Heated debates between liberal and conservative served to alienate some within the churches and to keep others away altogether.

Billy Sunday tried to avoid being closely identified with William Jennings Bryan and the militant creationist crowd associated with the Scopes trial, although his antievolutionist posture was well known. He tried even more strenuously to distance himself from the Ku Klux Klan, which was emerging in the cities and finding some favor among uneducated fundamentalists who had recently left the farms of the South and middle America. Nevertheless, many undiscerning observers associated Sunday with both groups.

The 1920s ushered in other changes that cut against the grain of Billy Sunday's spiritual goals. Disillusionment with the idealism of World War I and the prewar Wilsonian reform movement provoked an age of reaction. Everyone and everything associated with the war and prewar reform became suspect and out of fashion. Unfortunately for Sunday's religious agenda, he had identified himself with the reform movement through his ardent campaign for Prohibition—a cause that itself grew increasingly unpopular in the late 1920s and early 1930s. He was also inextricably identified with the moral crusade to "save the world for democracy" in World War I, a cause that was widely discredited during the twenties following revelations of the huge profits that industry had made off the great conflict.

And had his association with these two lost causes not been enough to hurt the old evangelist's image, his love affair with the Republican party—and especially with Herbert Hoover—would have done it. Republicanism was popular enough in the 1920s, but the stock market crash in 1929 and the ensuing Great Depression badly tarnished the Republican party's image, and Hoover was thoroughly discredited. Billy had diligently campaigned for Hoover in 1928, and men and women all over America had indelible images of Sunday standing in front of "Hoover for President" banners. The evangelist preached Hoover with all of the fervor that he preached repentance from sin—thereby himself playing no small role in the secularization of his own brand of religion. It is true that Billy Sunday distanced himself from Hoover by 1932, but by then the damage was done. In the minds of many, crusade evangelism was thoroughly politicized and hence distanced from the kingdom of God.

If we were to look at Billy Sunday solely from the perspective of his later years, we might see little more than a sad anachronism—an old-time preacher who had outlived his relevance. But a longer view gives us a much more complicated picture. In fact Billy Sunday powerfully influenced not only his own time but generations to come. Indeed, his influence continues into the late twentieth century. It is probably true, as his critics said, that many of the million trail hitters who went forward at his preaching services did so just to shake the famous preacher's hand, that some of those who hit the sawdust trail were merely responding to the emotion of the moment and were not ultimately changed by the experience. Yet the testimonies are legion of lives that were fundamentally and drastically changed for the good. Newspaper files and Sunday's letter files are replete with testimonies—many of them written years after the revival—from people whose marriages were saved, from drug addicts who left their addiction behind, from alcoholics who stopped drinking, from criminals who became preachers, and from people of every imaginable kind who left their lives of sin behind and became productive members of society.

In many of these cases those whose lives were markedly changed went on to point still others to a transforming Christian faith, so that the effect continues on in geometric proportions. One man who wrote to Billy Sunday in 1932, thanking him for leading him to Christ in 1914, noted that in the years since, he had gone to Asbury College, started a slum ministry in Lexington, Kentucky, and led many people to the faith. Billy also provided funds to give Chicago's Pacific Garden Mission a permanent endowment, and over seventy years later that institution, where Sunday himself was converted, continues to minister to countless men, women, and children.

It is also significant that in the wake of Billy Sunday's revivals, hundreds of evangelists and preachers fanned out all over the United States. The Rev. Jim Goodheart, for instance, a reformed alcoholic who became famous in Denver, Colorado, for helping the down-and-out find new life through faith in Christ, studied Sunday's theology, style, and methods. For years the director of the Denver Rescue Mission, Goodheart had an enormous impact on the central Rocky Mountain region during the years before the Great Depression. Likewise the Rev. John Brown, an evangelist who successfully traveled the South, imitated Sunday's approach, from sending an advance man ahead, setting up the facilities, organizing the services, and giving invitations, to selling postcards, hymnals, and books at the back of the tent or hall.

Both of the Sundays used their prestige to promote rescue missions and churches throughout the United States. They gave generously of their own money to several institutions, and they gave talks at countless fund-raising banquets to help even more. The range of influence of their ever-widening network was vast; it virtually spread from Mexico to Canada and from coast to coast.

Sunday's influence was also extended through clubs that were formed in the wake of his revivals. As soon as Virginia Asher joined the organization in 1912, she began organizing Business Women's Bible Clubs which met during the crusades and for years afterward. The purpose of these groups was to help the female converts grow in their newfound faith through regular fellowship with and accountability to mature Christian women. These clubs also became decidedly evangelistic, sponsoring luncheons and dinners designed to bring still more women into the fold. Virginia Asher not only launched these associations in every city where a revival was held but also did her best to stay in touch with the leadership of these groups until her death in 1937. She also continued to influence these women by urging them to come singly or with their families to summer Bible conferences at Winona Lake.

In the same vein as Asher's women's clubs, many of the men organized Businessmen's Evangelistic Clubs (sometimes dubbed Billy Sunday Clubs) in every city where a revival was held. Ten years after the formation of one such club in Charlotte, North Carolina, the membership sponsored a revival that produced over six thousand conversions—one of whom was a sixteen-year-old named Billy Graham. He was destined to go on and preach the gospel of Jesus Christ to more people than any other evangelist.

This passing of the torch from one generation to the next happened many times over, of course. In October 1986, at the Pacific Garden's 109th Anniversary Rally, the Rev. Jerry Falwell announced to the gathering that he was a "great-great grandson of the mission." Pacific Garden had "led Billy Sunday to Christ," he said, and Sunday had "led Fred Donnelson to Christ, who led Paul Donnelson to Christ, who led Jerry Falwell to Christ."

The impact of Billy Sunday's ministry cannot always be documented as in the Graham and Falwell cases. Indeed, during the first decade of the century the editor of the *Missouri Valley News* (Dunlap, Iowa) put it well when he wrote, "Mr. Sunday leaves town today, but his influence will remain for years to come. No one can measure its magnitude. Who can say how much trouble and grief have been averted by his coming?"

One area in which Billy Sunday made an unusual impact was black America. Conservative white Christians are often assumed to be indifferent to racial and social problems, but this was definitely not the case with the famous evangelist. From the beginning of his career as an evangelist and Bible teacher with the Chicago YMCA, he had a special place in his heart for the minorities and the poor, and he spent much time in their midst. This identification with the urban poor continued throughout his life with his support for urban missions. Furthermore, for a white man, he was unusually sensitive to the needs of blacks, and the black community responded to his message. After a campaign in

Kansas City, Missouri, the black press ran a bold headline, "Hail Billy Sunday." The paper's editor singled out Billy's "famous 'booze' sermon" for special praise: "to say we were hypnotized—enthralled—enchanted and reconverted anew is but feebly telling the whole truth." The editor also took note of the fact that Sunday had cared enough to go to a black church and preach. But he expressed his concern for the oppressed in more ways than this. He was vociferous in his attacks on child labor, for example, attacking the practice in a 1917 sermon in New York City entitled "Ye Must Be Born Again." He also was a persistent and outspoken supporter of women's suffrage.

Few white evangelists—indeed few white Christians even among the liberals—crossed the color line in those years. Calling for women's suffrage or an end to child labor was one thing, but scaling the barriers between the races was another matter. Almost everywhere Sunday went for a multiweek revival, there is evidence that he reached out to the black community. He held integrated services in Wichita and Kansas City when no one else considered doing so. And even when he went into the deep South, where evangelists were harassed by the law for holding racially mixed services and baptisms, he insisted on opening his meetings to all people.

On the heels of Billy's two-month crusade in Atlanta in December 1917, he received a letter from Lula Rhodes, a black woman from that city. She wrote to thank the evangelist and his staff for having remembered the blacks. He was the only white man besides President William Howard Taft ever to have worshiped in their church—and she confided that she had felt closer to Billy than she had to the ex-president: "You feel perfectly at home in his presence. He makes you feel so by his kind words and actions." Rhodes was impressed with Billy's attitude toward their worship service. He was not in the least bit patronizing or condescending. The congregation enjoyed "seeing Mr. Sunday so much impressed with our singing and way of worshipping," she wrote. "We are just as sincere in it as he is in his way, and I believe he looks at it in that way." In the end, she said, "Mr. Sunday has knocked off more bumps, has filled in more ditches, cleaned up more new ground since he has been in Atlanta than anyone else since Lincoln signed freedom."

The Rhodes letter contained still more insights about Billy Sunday and the segregation problem in Atlanta. It seems that Billy had accepted an invitation for coffee at the home of a prominent white minister, and, predictably, he was entertained only by white people. But as Jesus knew that Zacchaeus yearned to see him, she wrote, Billy Sunday knew there were blacks in the house who wanted to see him. And, as Jesus had gone out of his way to encounter Zacchaeus, Sunday went out of his way to see his admirers. He asked the pastor for permission to go to the kitchen and thank those who had prepared the delicious coffee. After complimenting the cook, he took time to talk with the entire black household staff who had gathered in the kitchen. Rhodes also recalled an occasion on which Sunday had taken three little black boys up on the platform at one of his meetings and shown an unself-conscious affection toward them. "He was so kind to those young boys that every colored child will listen to his message now."

Actions such as those in Atlanta had a profound impact on at least part of black America. Not a few blacks became Billy Sunday boosters. At least one black evangelist, the Rev. Solomon Lightfoot Michaux, proudly proclaimed himself "the colored Billy Sunday."

That Sunday was a hit with blacks was nowhere more clearly demonstrated than during his early 1930 revival in Wichita. He had support from both whites and blacks in that Kansas community, and he held racially mixed meetings there. The white turnout was only moderate, but blacks came in large numbers, and he was delighted to tell Nell that "you never heard such shouting."

Minorities other than Afro-Americans also supported Billy Sunday and were evidently encouraged by his ministry. Although it was commonly said that immigrants, especially those from southern and eastern Europe, had little to do with

Billy Sunday, there is some evidence to the contrary. For example, we know that an Italian-American priest urged his parish of Roman Catholics—mostly Italian miners—to attend Billy's autumn 1909 meetings in Boulder, Colorado. And many conservative Catholics applauded his attacks on socialism, communism, and assorted varieties of radicalism. They also seconded his vitriolic assault on the evolutionists—especially Christian evolutionists—who belittled William Jennings Bryan and others who supported a literalist reading of the Genesis account of creation. And in several sermons, Sunday took to task conservative Christians who misused their time and energy criticizing faithful Roman Catholics—fellow believers who worshiped and followed Christ.

It surprised and disappointed some conservative Protestants that Sunday sought and attained the support of Roman Catholics, and many were even more stunned by his staunch defense of Jews. In an impassioned sermon in Omaha in 1915 he denounced anti-Semitism. How can Gentiles think they will win God's favor by criticizing the Jews, he wanted to know. They are God's chosen people, Billy insisted, and he will always bless them in special ways.

And so we see that Billy Sunday was no living anachronism when it came to his views on minorities, women's rights, and child labor legislation. He was forward-looking as well with respect to unity among Christian denominations. No one did more to promote the church union movement in urban America than the itinerant evangelist. He called for the creation of an evangelistic association in every city where he preached. He always sought to include the pastors of all the churches among the members of this body. Unity in Christ—along the lines of John 17:20-23—was Sunday's hope for each community where he held a long revival. Seldom did every church back his meetings, but in all the largest cities at least a majority of the ministers rallied behind the crusade. He found most support from the conservative churches, to be sure, and least support from the sacramentalist churches such as the Episcopalians, Lutherans, and Roman Catholics. From time to time, though, some of the high church leaders caught Sunday's enthusiasm for a united Christendom. They led their churches into his mainstream evangelistic effort even if they were tentative about his style and his emphasis on conversion.

In 1932 the Rev. Walter Bennett, an Episcopal priest at Trinity Church in Lowville, New York, wrote a repentant letter to the aging evangelist. Fr. Bennett confessed that few of his Episcopalian colleagues had positive things to say about Billy Sunday. He admitted that he himself had preached sermons against Sunday during his revivals in Colorado in the early years of the century and had slandered the traveling evangelist on other occasions as well. But one night while he was staying in a Rocky Mountain hotel with a diverse group of ministers, he made a snide remark to the men about the Rev. Billy Sunday, and, wrote Bennett, a Presbyterian divine really brought me down. "Never speak against any man like Mr. Sunday who God is using as he is using him. God used Samson although by no means perfect. God is with Billy." Bennett professed that "Nothing but praise has ever passed my lips since of Billy Sunday." He acknowledged that "long ago I learned that he was a bigger and better man than I am and slurs on a fellow workman, no matter how different his message and methods may be, surely do not become any minister of God." He concluded by saying "Be his theology what it may, his energy, his devotion, his will, his love of Christ, his sincerity, his great humanness make his story about as interesting as words can be."

In the final analysis, whatever else can be said about the Billy Sunday legacy, one thing needs to be stressed. Through his preaching and teaching, through his inauguration of Billy Sunday clubs all over urban America, and through his zealous promotion of Bible conferences such as those at Winona Lake, he did more than anyone else in the first half of the twentieth century to keep biblical Christianity vital. His commitment to Christian unity and some social issues put him at loggerheads with some in the growing fundamentalist movement, and his unswerving allegiance to a conservative interpretation of the Bible put him at odds with many in the liberal seminaries and churches, but no amount of criticism from either side ever shook his single-minded loyalty to God the Father, Son, and Holy Spirit or his abiding love for the church of Christ, and no one can deny that he persuaded and emboldened many Christians to stand with him on this sure ground.

Afterword

1935-1957

"Billy was my job."

Before the undertaker took Billy Sunday's body away, Nell laid her head on his arm and prayed, "Lord, if there's anything left in the world for me to do, if you'll let me know about it, I want to promise you that I'll try to do it the best I know how."

In her autobiography she told a friend, "I didn't see one single thing left for me to do! Billy was my job. We had lived together for forty-seven years—we had traveled together for thirty-nine years in the work—and he was *gone!* There just didn't seem to be anything left for me to do! So I prayed that prayer to God." Two days later she was reminded of this heaven-directed petition when some men from New York who had been greatly influenced by Billy's ministry showed up for the funeral. The day before the service they asked Mrs. Sunday if she would consider going out to New York to speak at memorial services for him on November 19. Her first reaction "was to scream at them and say, 'No!' You've no business asking me now. This isn't the time for it, or for me to promise to go! Billy isn't even buried yet!" It also occurred to her that the nineteenth was Billy's birthday. But then her prayer of two days earlier blazed into her mind. "Why, certainly! Why not? Of course!"

The affirmative response to an invitation to speak was the prelude to twenty-two years of active ministry. Helen Amelia "Nell" Sunday was in New York on November 19, 1935, preaching the gospel of Jesus Christ, eulogizing her husband, and encouraging Christians to grow in their faith. From that day until her death she was not without invitations to speak. All alone she carried on the aggressive ministry she had begun with her husband.

The years without Billy were full and challenging. She did evangelistic preaching, spoke at conferences, and was frequently on the platform of evangelistic crusades giving a testimony before the sermon. Among the famous evangelists who visited her at Winona Lake and urged her to join them on their own revival platforms was Billy Graham from North Carolina.

Nell obliged Billy Graham and a host of lesser-known preachers, and she also gave generously of her time to numerous urban ministries. She gave talks at fund-raising dinners for Chicago's Pacific Garden Mission, the Denver Rescue Mission in Colorado, and many other urban missions. She also contributed considerable time and energy to the Winona Lake Christian Assembly, speaking and helping raise money for its work.

"Ma" Sunday, as many of her friends still called her, not only helped raise money for various organizations but also gave away much of the money she and Billy had left at the time of his death. Her correspondence files are full of evidence that she gave large donations to favorite ministries, such as Pacific Garden Mission, Winona Lake Christian Assembly, and Bob Jones College. A host of other charities tapped her generous nature as well.

The years of solitary ministry were fulfilling, but they were not without heartache and adversity. If the loss of two children and her husband was not enough cause for grief, she buried her remaining two children within nine years of Billy's death. William Ashley Jr. died in 1938 at the age of thirty-seven, and the youngest child, Paul, passed away in 1944 at the age of thirty-three.

Four years later, in 1948, Nell suffered a heart attack, but before long she was back on the circuit doing the work of an evangelist. Wherever she went she spoke about her two favorite subjects—Billy Sunday and Jesus Christ. Just before her death—she was eighty-eight years old—she granted a historian permission to tape-record a two-hour interview. In it she praised God for the years she and Billy had together, and she cited many examples of the effects of his preaching. Still active and alert, she reminded the historian that Americans who travel to the far-flung Christian mission stations of the world continually encounter missionaries who say they were converted at Billy Sunday revival meetings. She also reflected on the world's problems: "Nothing but Jesus Christ is going to do—is going to provide the remedy of the world's ills today."

Always reminiscing about her husband and then pointing to Jesus Christ, "Ma" Sunday concluded with a word of encouragement for the younger people she was passing the torch to:

> I'm so glad that the young men, like Billy Graham, Merv Rosell, Jack Schuler, Jimmy Johnson, and oh, a whole lot of others that I can't mention right now, are on the job, night and day, out preaching God's blessed Word and giving out the invitation to come and accept him. And I'm glad that God has let me do my little here and there. . . . And now I'll say, "Goodnight! Goodby!"

That was 1956. On February 20, 1957, she died while visiting her grandson Paul Haines in Arizona.

Notes on Sources

In the introduction to this book I note that in writing it I have adopted a point of view less enthusiastic toward Billy Sunday than the laudatory older biographers. Nevertheless, these older works—Elijah P. Brown's *The Real Billy Sunday* (New York: Fleming H. Revell, 1914), William T. Ellis's *"Billy" Sunday: The Man and His Message* (Philadelphia: John C. Winston, 1914), and Lee Thomas's *The Billy Sunday Story* (Grand Rapids: Zondervan, 1961)—all contain much useful information, and I am indebted to them. I relied upon all three biographies as well as Billy Sunday's *Autobiography*, reprinted in the 1936 edition of William T. Ellis's *"Billy" Sunday*. Nell Sunday's little autobiography, *Ma Sunday Still Speaks* (Winona Lake, Ind.: Winona Lake Christian Assembly, 1957), and Homer Rodeheaver's *Twenty Years with Billy Sunday* (Nashville: Cokesbury Press, 1936) were also extremely useful, as was William G. McLoughlin Jr.'s rather critical book, *Billy Sunday Was His Real Name* (Chicago: University of Chicago Press, 1955). McLoughlin's work is a model study of the structure and function of Sunday's evangelistic organization. He embraces the biases of the progressive historians of the first half of this century, and as a consequence assumes Sunday to be, either consciously or unconsciously, a part of a collective capitalist conspiracy against the working class. Although I do not agree with McLoughlin's angle of vision or his anti-Sunday posture, I immensely admire his scholarship, and his book was a key source for me.

It will be clear to anyone who reads Douglas W. Frank's *Less Than Conquerors: How Evangelicals Entered the Twentieth Century* (Grand Rapids: Eerdmans, 1986), that I admire Billy Sunday a good deal more than Prof. Frank does. But differences in our basic assumptions about the evangelist notwithstanding, I found Frank's book to be intelligent and helpful. A bit of a prophet himself, Frank helped me think through many things, and I hope he helped keep me honest. Frank and I disagree most on the extent to which we see Sunday's ministry (and the teachings of the Keswick movement) as a response to the pluralism of urban industrialism. Frank argues that Sunday and others like him shaped their theology to fit their times and respond to their opponents. I agree to an extent, but I believe he went beyond mere reaction. I would contend that Billy Sunday was a true biblicist, not a culture Christian. Historian Stephen Barabas sees in the Keswick movement an attempt to reassert Pauline theology, especially as it relates to holiness and sanctification, and I would put Sunday in this camp. On the same grounds, I disagree with Frank's characterization of the Victorious Life movement, of which Sunday was a part, as a modern sociological phenomenon. I would argue that it was Pauline after the fashion of the Keswick movement, that it was just one of many reform attempts that have surfaced during two thousand years of church history.

No one can write on my subject without benefiting from William G. McLoughlin's *Revivals, Awakenings, and Reform* (Chicago: University of Chicago Press, 1978), George M. Marsden's *Fundamentalism and American Culture: The Shaping of Twentieth-Century Evangelicalism, 1870-1925* (New York: Oxford University Press, 1980), and William R. Hutchison's *The Modernist Im-*

pulse in American Protestantism (Cambridge: Harvard University Press, 1976). Two other books helped me see the Sunday era in perspective: Lewis Atherton's *Main Street on the Middle Border* (Bloomington, Ind.: Indiana University Press, 1954) and Aimee Semple McPherson's *The Story of My Life* (Hollywood: Echo Park Evangelistic Association, 1951).

There is absolutely no way I could have written the book I have—with its emphasis on Billy Sunday's personality and family life—without the Sunday Family Papers. I consulted the microfilm edition of "The Papers of William and Helen Sunday," located in the Archives of the Billy Graham Center, Wheaton College, Wheaton, Illinois. In fact, this microfilm record, the use of which is greatly enhanced by Robert Shuster's *Guide to the Microfilm Edition*, is the backbone of this book. Perhaps eighty to ninety percent of my sources come from the Sunday papers and other unpublished primary sources such as newspapers, photographs, and U.S. Census data. The *New York Times* was illuminating, as were scores of articles from the popular magazines of Sunday's era.

For students of Billy Sunday, I am obligated to provide some notes on my sources for each chapter.

Chapter One: Here I relied upon U.S. Census data and *A Hand Book of Iowa*, published by the Iowa Columbia Commission in 1893, both of which provide data on the places where Billy Sunday grew up. Sunday's *Autobiography* was likewise invaluable.

Chapter Two: Elijah Brown's *The Real Billy Sunday* and *Ma Sunday Still Speaks* both supply rich reminiscences and quotations from the "Pop" Anson baseball era. Besides these primary sources, two important secondary works, David Quentin Voight's *American Baseball: From Gentleman's Sport to the Commissioner System* (University Park, Pa.: Pennsylvania State University Press, 1983) and Harold Seymour's *Baseball: The Early Years* (New York: Oxford University Press, 1960), were extremely helpful. I also drew on Mel Larson's *Ten Famous Christian Athletes* (Grand Rapids: Zondervan, 1958) and *The Baseball Ency-*

clopedia, 4th ed. (New York: Macmillan, 1979), edited by Joseph L. Reichler.

For information on Sunday's conversion, I relied chiefly on his autobiography and Helen Sunday's reminiscences. They both say they met in 1886 after his conversion, whereas McLoughlin says 1885. In the context of Sunday's conversion I consulted Carl F. H. Henry's *The Pacific Garden Mission: A Doorway to Heaven* (Grand Rapids: Zondervan, 1942).

Regarding the YMCA, I consulted C. Howard Hopkins's *History of the Y.M.C.A. in North America* (New York: Association Press, 1951).

Chapter Three: Information about Sunday's early YMCA work was drawn from the Brown and Ellis biographies and both of the Sundays' autobiographies.

I drew on the same four sources regarding the J. Wilbur Chapman era as well as Ford C. Ottman's *J. Wilbur Chapman: A Biography* (Garden City, N.Y.: Doubleday, 1920). Chapter 1 of McLoughlin's *Billy Sunday* also contains material on Chapman and Sunday in the 1890s, as do newspaper clippings in the Sunday Papers.

Recollections about Garner, Iowa, came from *Ma Sunday Still Speaks* and Brown's biography.

Chapter Four: In this chapter I began my heavy reliance on the microfilm record of the Sunday family correspondence in the Billy Graham Center Archives. McLoughlin also provides helpful material on the early Sunday revivals, and Brown has indispensable material.

I garnered additional background material for this chapter from the U.S. Census, Fred A. Shannon's *The Farmer's Last Frontier: Agriculture, 1860-1897* (New York: Farrar & Rinehart, 1945), and Lewis Atherton's *Main Street on the Middle Border*.

Sermon quotations are taken from the Sunday Family Papers files, William A. Sunday's *Wonderful and Other Sermons* (Winona Lake, Ind.: Winona Lake Christian Academy, n.d.), *Billy Sunday Speaks* (Grand Rapids: Zondervan, 1937), and Elijah P. Brown's *The Real Billy Sunday*.

Material on Sunday's ordination is taken from his *Autobiography* and the Ellis, Brown, and McLoughlin volumes.

For a comparison of my views of the Keswick and Victorious Life movements with those of Douglas Frank, see *Less Than Conquerors* and Stephen Barabas's *So Great Salvation: The History and Message of the Keswick Convention* (London: Marshall, Morgan & Scott, 1952).

Chapter Five: Robert Shuster's *Guide to the Microfilm Edition of the Sunday Family Papers* includes a chronological list of the cities where Sunday preached. The U.S. Census enabled me to trace the size of these places for the dates Sunday was there.

Income data comes from Arthur S. Link's *American Epoch: A History of the United States since the 1890's*, vol. 1 (New York: Knopf, 1955).

I relied heavily on letters and sermons in the Sunday Papers for this chapter. I also used two other Billy Graham Center Archival collections: Papers of Virginia Asher, and extensive photograph files of Sunday and his team members.

The Fisher Family Papers, Wheaton College Archives and Special Collections, were helpful, as was an unpublished Ph.D. dissertation by Maynard D. Hilgendorf entitled "Billy Sunday: 'I am Glad I Came to Detroit'—A Study of Rhetorical Strategies in the 1916 Campaign" (University of Michigan, 1985).

On Sunday's attempts to promote racial harmony I used material in the clipping files of the Sunday Papers. Especially helpful with regard to the Atlanta campaign were clippings from *Current Opinion* (March 1918) and *The Continent* (Nov. 29, 1917).

On Sunday's finances, I consulted McLoughlin (especially chapter 3) but drew most heavily on the Sunday Papers, which are rich with data.

On music in the campaigns, I consulted Rodeheaver's *Twenty Years with Billy Sunday* and Richard Crabb's *Radio's Beautiful Day* (Wheaton, Ill.: DuPage Heritage Gallery, 1982).

Chapter Six: Among my sources for this chapter is the personal library of William A. Sunday in the Sunday home at

Winona Lake, Indiana. I am also grateful to the Rev. Jerry Root of Wheaton, Illinois, who gave me a copy of E. M. Bounds's *Satan: His Personality, Power, and Overthrow* (Chicago: Fleming H. Revell, 1922) from his personal library—the presentation copy given to Billy Sunday, complete with Sunday's underlinings.

Letters between Billy and Nell reveal their agony over the deaths of Helen, George, and Nora, as well as issues surrounding the illnesses both suffered.

McLoughlin has much good material on the opposition Sunday received, especially from Rabbi Wise and George Creel.

Financial records are interspersed in the Sunday Papers. Rodeheaver's letters to Mrs. Sunday and Billy are in the Sunday Papers—specifically the letters dated July 3, 1927, and October 20, 1929. Rodeheaver's *Twenty Years* is also illuminating on the criticisms.

Mrs. Sunday described the last week before Billy's death in some detail to Lee Thomas, who recorded the information in *The Billy Sunday Story*. I also drew on her autobiography in this regard.

Chapter Seven: An obituary and descriptions of the Sunday funeral service appeared in the *Chicago Tribune* in November 1935. See also chapter 23 of Lee Thomas's biography. And *Ma Sunday Still Speaks* contains some excellent illustrative material.

Rodeheaver comments on Sunday's clothing and habits in *Twenty Years,* and the newspaper clippings in the Sunday Papers are replete with material on local color.

For sources on James Goodheart, see my book *The Denver Rescue Mission: A History* (Denver, Colo.: The Denver Rescue Mission, 1983). The John Brown material comes from the Clyde S. Kilby Papers in the Marion E. Wade Center, Wheaton College, Wheaton, Illinois.

The connection between Billy Sunday, Mordecai Ham, and Billy Graham is made in a 1949 letter to Mrs. Sunday from Ham in the Sunday Papers. There is more material on this subject in Edward E. Ham's *The Story of an All-Day Prayer Meet-*

ing and the Revival when Billy Graham Found Christ (Grand Rapids: Zondervan, 1953). Helpful, too, is Earle E. Cairns's *An Endless Line of Splendor: Revivals and Their Leaders from the Great Awakening to the Present* (Wheaton, Ill.: Tyndale House, 1986). Jerry Falwell's address is recorded in the *Pacific Garden News* (January 1987).

Material on Sunday's attitude toward Roman Catholics and Jews was taken from the Sunday Family Papers, both letters and sermons.

Material on Sunday's relationship with blacks was taken from the Sunday Papers as well as from an Afro-American newspaper, *The Kansas City [Missouri] Sun*, for 1916 and the *Dictionary of American Negro Biography*, edited by Rayford W. Logan and Michael R. Winston (New York: W. W. Norton, 1982), which contains a sketch of S. L. Michaux.

The William Jennings Bryan Papers in the Library of Congress gave me some excellent insights on Bryan and the controversies surrounding the Scopes trial and the creationist-evolutionist controversy in general. On the Ku Klux Klan in this era, I consulted Kenneth Jackson's *The Ku Klux Klan in the City, 1915-1930* (New York: Oxford University Press, 1967).

Afterword: For the material in this brief section, I drew on Mrs. Sunday's papers in the Sunday Family Papers as well as her autobiography and Lee Thomas's biography, *The Billy Sunday Story*.

Appendix

Two of the sermons Billy Sunday delivered most often are reproduced here in their entirety. The substance of both messages dates to the 1910s, but he delivered each countless times in slightly altered forms until his death in 1935.

My studies have shown that although Sunday's sermons are quoted in almost every book written about him or his ministry, his words are frequently taken out of context.

These two texts—one rather brief and the other quite long—reflect the diversity of his preaching goals and style. From these sermons the reader can get a glimpse of his sources and assumptions, as well as his theology, biases, and style. They give evidence of a preacher who was decidedly more complex and gifted than his many critics have claimed.

Heaven

Everybody wants to go to Heaven.
    We are all curious.
    We want to know:

        Where heaven is,
        How it looks,
        Who are there,
        What they wear,
        And how to get there:

Some say:
Heaven is a state or a condition. You are wrong.
Your home is not a state or a condition. It is a place.
The penitentiary is not a state or a condition. It is a place.
Jesus said:
    "I go to prepare a place for you that where I am ye may be also."
    The only source of information we have about Heaven is the Bible.

It tells us:

That God's throne is in the heavens and that the earth is His footstool. And if our spiritual visions are not blinded we believe it is true.

Enoch walked with God and was not—for God took him to Heaven. He left this earth at the behest of God and went to Heaven where God has His dwelling place.

Elijah, when his mission on earth was finished, in the providence of God, was wafted to Heaven in a chariot of fire. The former pupils went out to search for the translated Prophet but they did not find him.

But it was the privilege of Peter, James, and John on the Mount of Transfiguration with Jesus to see the gates of Heaven open and two spirits jump down on the earth whom they recognized as Moses and Elijah who so many years before had walked through Palestine and warned the people of their sins and he slew 450 of the false prophets of Baal.

When Jesus began His public ministry we are told the heavens opened and God stopped making worlds and said from Heaven:

"This is My beloved Son. Hear ye Him."

Then Stephen, with his face lit up with the glories of the Celestial Kingdom as he looked steadfastly toward Heaven, saw it open. And Jesus Himself was standing at the right hand of God, the place He had designated before His Crucifixion and Resurrection would be His abiding place until the time of the Gentiles should be fulfilled, when He would leave Heaven with a shout of triumph and return to this earth in the clouds of Heaven.

Among the last declarations of Jesus, in which we all find so much comfort in the hour of bereavement, is:

"In My Father's house are many mansions: if it were not so I would have told you."

When Heaven's music burst upon human ears that first Christmas morning while the shepherds guarded their flocks on the moonlit hills of Judea, as the angels sang:

"Peace on Earth, good will to men, for unto you is born this day in the City of David a Saviour Who is Christ the Lord."
We have ample proof that Heaven is a real place.

> "When you have been there
> Ten thousand years—bright, shining like the sun—
> You'll have no less days,
> To sing God's praise,
> Than when you first begun."

Oh, what a place Heaven is—the Tuileries of the French, the Windsor Castle of the English, the Alhambra of the Spanish, the Schonbrunn of the Austrians, the White House of the United States—these are all dungeons compared with Heaven.

There are mansions there for all the redeemed—one for the martyrs with blood-red robes; one for you ransomed from sin; one for me plucked like a brand from the fire.

Look and see—who are climbing the golden stairs, who are walking the golden streets, who are looking out of the windows?

Some whom we knew and loved here on earth.

Yes, I know them.

My father and mother, blithe and young as they were on their wedding day.

Our son and our daughter, sweet as they were when they cuddled down to sleep in our arms.

My brother and sister, merrier than when we romped and roamed the fields and plucked wild flowers and listened to the whippoorwill as he sang his lonesome song away over in Sleepy Hollow on the old farm in Iowa where we were born and reared.

Cough, gone—cancer, gone—consumption, gone—erysipelas, gone—blindness, gone—rheumatism, gone—lameness, gone—asthma, gone—tears, gone—groans, sighs, gone—sleepless nights, gone.

I think it will take some of us a long time to get used to Heaven.

Fruits without one speck upon them.
Pastures without one thistle or weed.
Orchestra without one discord.
Violin without a broken string.
Harps all in tune.
The river without a torn or overflowed bank.
The sunrise and sunset swallowed up in the Eternal Day.
"For there shall be no night there."
Heaven will be free from all that curses us here.
No sin—no sorrow—no poverty—no sickness—no pain—no want—no aching heads or hearts—no war—no death.
No watching the undertaker screw the coffin-lid over our loved ones.

When I reach Heaven I won't stop to look for Abraham, Isaac, Jacob, Moses, Joseph, David, Daniel, Peter or Paul.

I will rush past them all saying, "Where is Jesus? I want to see Jesus who saved my soul one dark stormy night in Chicago in 1887."

If we could get a real appreciation of what Heaven is we would all be so homesick for Heaven the devil wouldn't have a friend left on earth.

The Bible's description of Heaven is: the length and the breadth and the height of it are equal.

I sat down and took 12 inches for a foot, our standard. That would make it two thousand five hundred miles long, two thousand five hundred miles wide, two thousand five hundred miles high. Made of pure gold like glass. Twelve gates, each gate made of one pearl. The foundations are of precious stones. Imagine eight thousand miles of diamonds, rubies, sapphires, emeralds, topaz, amethysts, jade, garnets.

Some one may say:
"Well, that will be pleasant, if true."
Another says:
"I hope it's true";
"Perhaps it's true";
"I wish it were true."

It is true!

The kiss of reunion at the gate of Heaven is as certain as the goodbye kiss when you drift out with the tide.

> "God holds the key
> Of all unknown,
> And I am glad.
> If other hands should hold the key,
> Or if He trusted it to me,
> I might be sad."

Death is a cruel enemy. He robs the mother of her baby, the wife of her husband, the parents of their children, the lover of his intended wife. He robs the lodge of its members, the Nation of its President.

Death is a rude enemy. He upsets our best plans without an apology. He enters the most exclusive circles without an invitation.

Death is an international enemy. There is no nation which he does not visit. The islands of the seas where the black skinned mothers rock their babies to sleep to the lullaby of the ocean's waves. The restless sea. The majestic mountains. All are his haunts.

Death is an untiring enemy. He continues his ghastly work Spring, Summer, Autumn and Winter. He never tires in his ceaseless rounds, gathering his spoils of human souls.

But Death is a vanquished enemy. Jesus arose from the dead and abolished death although we may be called upon to die.

Death to the Christian is swinging open the door through which he passes into Heaven.

"Aren't you afraid?" said the wife to a dying miner.

"Afraid, Lassie. Why should I be? I know Jesus and Jesus knows me."

This house in which we live, "our body," is beginning to lean. The windows rattle. The glass is dim. The shingles are falling off.

You will reach the river's brink,
Some sweet day, bye and bye.
You will clasp your broken link
Some sweet day, bye and bye.

There's a glorious kingdom waiting
In the land beyond the sky,
Where the Saints have been gathering
Year by year.

And the days are swiftly passing
That shall bring the Kingdom night,
For the coming of the Lord
Draweth near.

Thank God for the rainbow of hope that bends above the graves of our loved ones.

We stand on this side of the grave and mourn as they go.
They stand on the other side and rejoice as they come.

On the Resurrection morning
Soul and body meet again.
No more sorrow, no more weeping,
No more pain.

Soul and body reunited.
Thenceforth nothing can divide.
Waking up in Christ's own likeness;
Satisfied!

On that happy Easter morning,
All the graves their dead restore.
Father, sister, child and mother,
Meet once more.

To that brightest of all meetings
Brings us Jesus Christ, at last,
By thy cross through death and judgment,
Holding fast.

The Bible indicates that angels know each other. If they have the power to recognize each other, won't we?

The Bible describes Heaven as a great home circle. It would be a queer home circle if we did not know each other.

The Bible describes death as a sleep. Well, we know each other before we go to sleep and we know each other when we wake up. Do you imagine we will be bigger fools in Heaven than we are here on earth?

A woman lay dying. She had closed her eyes. Her sister, thinking her dead, commenced the wail of mourning. The dying woman raised her hand and said:

"Hush! Hush! I am listening to the breezes waving the branches in the trees of life."

You will be through with your back-biting enemies. They will call you vile names no more. They will no longer misrepresent your good deeds.

Broken hearts will be bound up. Wounds will be healed. Sorrows ended.

The comfort of God is greater than the sorrows of men. I've thanked God a thousand times for the roses but never for the thorns, but now I have learned to thank Him for the thorns.

You will never be sick again. Never be tired again. Never weep again.

What's the use of fretting when we are on our way to such a coronation.

You must know the password if you ever enter Heaven, Jesus said,

"I am the Way, the Truth and the Life. No man cometh unto the Father but by Me."

Here comes a crowd.

They cry:

"Let me in. I was very useful on earth. I built churches. I endowed colleges. I was famous for my charities. I have done many wonderful things."

"I never knew you."

Another crowd shouts:

"We were highly honored on earth. The world bowed very low before us. Now we have come to get our honors in Heaven."

175

"We never knew you."

Another crowd shouts:

"We were very moral. We never lied, swore or got drunk."

"We never knew you."

Another crowd approaches and says:

"We were sinners, wanderers from God. We have come up, not because we deserve Heaven, but because we heard of the saving power of Jesus, and we have accepted Him as our Saviour."

They all cry, "Jesus, Jesus. Thou Son of God, open to us."

They all pass through the pearly gates.

One step this side and you are paupers for eternity. One step on the other side and you are kings and queens for eternity.

When I think of Heaven and my entering it I feel awkward.

Sometimes when I have been exposed to the weather, shoes covered with mud, coat wet and soiled with mud and rain, hair disheveled, I feel I am not fit to go in and sit among the well dressed guests.

So I feel that way about Heaven. I need to be washed in the blood of the Lamb and clothed in the robe of Christ's righteousness. I need the pardoning waves of God's mercy to roll over my soul. And thank God, they have.

If you go first will you come down half way and meet me between the willow banks of earth and the palm groves of Heaven? You who have loved ones in Heaven, will you take a pledge with me to meet them when the day dawns and the shadows flee away?

Some who read this are sadly marching into the face of the setting sun. You are sitting by the window of your soul looking out toward the twilight of life's purple glow. You are listening to the music of the breaking waves of life's ebbing tide and longing for the sight of faces and the sound of voices loved and lost a while.

But if you are true to God and have accepted Jesus as your Saviour at last you will hail the coming morning radiant and glorious when the waves of the sea will become crystal chords in the grand organ of Eternity.

A saint lay dying. She said:

"My faith is being tried. The brightness of which you speak I do not have. But I have accepted Jesus as my Saviour and if God wishes to put me to sleep in the dark His will be done."

Sorrow sometimes plays strange dirges on the heartstrings of life before they break but the music always has a message of hope.

Should You Go First

Should you go first, and I remain
To walk the road alone,
I'll live in memory's garden, dear,
With happy days we've known.

In Spring I'll watch for roses red,
When fade the lilacs blue;
In early Fall, when brown leaves fall,
I'll catch a breath of you.

Should you go first, and I remain
For battles to be fought,
Each thing you've touched along the way
Will be a hallowed spot.

I'll hear your voice, I'll see you smile,
Though blindly I may grope;
The memory of your helping hand
Will buoy me on with hope.

Should you go first, and I remain
To finish with the scroll,
No length'ning shadows shall creep in
To make this life seem droll.

We've known so much of happiness,
We've had our cup of joy;
Ah, memory is one gift of God
That death cannot destroy.

Should you go first, and I remain,
One thing I'd have you do;
Walk slowly down the path of death,
For soon I'll follow you.

I'll want to know each step you take,
That I may walk the same;
For some day—down that lonely road—
You'll hear me call your name.

A. K. Rowswell (Rosey)

One day when the children were young I was romping and playing with them and I grew tired and lay down to rest. Half asleep and half awake I dreamed I journeyed to a far-off land.

It was not Persia, although the Oriental beauty and splendor were there.

It was not India, although the coral strands were there.

It was not Ceylon, although the beauty and spicy perfume of that famous island paradise were there.

It was not Italy, although the dreamy haze of the blue Italian sky beat above me.

It was not California nor Florida, although the soft flower-ladened breezes of the Pacific and the Atlantic were there.

I looked for weeds, briars, thorns and thistles, but I found none.

I saw the sun in all his meridian glory. I asked

"When will the sun set and it grow dark?"

They said:

"Oh, it never grows dark in this land. There is no night here. Jesus is the light."

I saw the people all clothed in holiday attire with faces wreathed in smiles and halos of glory about their heads.

I asked:

"When will the working men go by with calloused hands and empty dinner buckets and faces grimed with dust and toil?"

They said:

"Oh, we toil not, neither do we sow nor reap in this land."

I strolled out into the suburbs and the hills which would be a fit resting place for the dead to sleep. I looked for monuments, mausoleums, marble slabs, tombs and graves, but I saw none. I did see towers, spires and minarets.

I asked:

"Where do you bury the dead of this great city? Where are the grave-diggers? Where are the hearses that haul the dead to their graves?"

They said:

"Oh, we are never sick. None ever die in this land."

I asked:

"Where do the poor people live? Where are the homes of penury and want?"

They said:

"Oh, there are no poor in this land. There is no want here. None are ever hungry here."

I was puzzled.

I looked and saw a river. Its waves were breaking against golden and jewel strewn beaches.

I saw ships with sails of pure silk, bows covered with gold, oars tipped with silver.

I looked and saw a great multitude no man could number, rushing out of jungles of roses, down banks of violets, redolent of eternal Spring, pulsing with bird song and the voices of angels.

I realized Time had ended and Eternity had dawned.

I cried:

"Are all here?"

They echoed:

"Yes, all here."

And tower and spire and minaret all caroled my welcome home. And we all went leaping and singing and shouting the eternal praises of

God the Father,

God the Son,

God the Holy Spirit.

Home, home, at last!

BILLY SUNDAY

Here's to you, my friends.
May you live a hundred years,
Just to help us
Through this vale of tears.
May I live a hundred years
Short just one day,
Because I don't want to be here
After all my friends have gone away.

Get on the Water Wagon

I am the sworn, eternal, uncompromising enemy of the Liquor Traffic. I ask no quarter and I give none. I have drawn the sword in defense of God, home, wife, children and native land, and I will never sheathe it until the undertaker pumps me full of embalming fluid, and if my wife is alive, I think I shall call her to my bedside and say: "Nell, when I am dead, send for the butcher and skin me, and have my hide tanned and made into drum heads, and hire men to go up and down the land and beat the drums and say, 'My husband, "Bill" Sunday still lives and gives the whiskey gang a run for its money.' "

After all is said that can be said on the open licensed saloon, its degrading influence upon the individual, upon business, upon public morals, upon the home (for the time is long gone by when there is any grounds for argument, even its friends are forced to admit its vile corruption) there is one prime reason why the saloon has not been driven from the land long ago— that is the lying argument that saloons are needed to lighten taxes. I challenge you to show me any community, where a saloon license policy has lightened taxes.

Seventy-five per cent of our idiots came from intemperate parents. There are more insane people in the United States than students in the universities and colleges. In Kansas there are eighty-one counties without an insane man or woman. There are fifty-four counties that have no feeble-minded. Eighty per cent of the paupers are whiskey-made paupers. In Kansas there is only one pauper to every three thousand of the population. There are thirty-eight counties without a pauper; there are eighteen counties, which do not even own a farm for the poor; there are only six hundred paupers in the state.

Ninety per cent of our adult criminals are drinking men, and committed their crimes while under the influence of Booze.

In 1914 there were sixty-five counties in Kansas, with no prisoners in their jails. In some counties they have not called a Grand Jury to try a charge in ten years.

The people have over $200,000,000 on deposit in the banks. The death rate is the smallest in the world—seven out of every one thousand of the population.

In the state of Massachusetts in ten years, the yearly average of crime has been 32,639 cases, and 31,978 have been caused by drink. The Chicago *Tribune* kept track of the number of murders committed in the saloons in ten years and the number was 53,436.

Archbishop Ireland said, "I find social crime and ask what caused it? They say 'drink!' I find poverty. What caused it? 'Drink!' I find families broken up and ask what caused it, they tell me 'drink!' I find men behind prison bars and ask, 'what put you here?' They say 'drink.' I stand by the scaffold and ask, 'What made you a murderer?' They cry 'drink! drink!' "

"If God would place in my hand a wand with which to dispel the evils of temperance, I would strike at the door of every brewery, and every distillery, and every saloon until the accursed traffic was driven from the land."

The saloon is the sum of all villainies. It is worse than war, worse than pestilence, worse than famine. It is the crime of crimes. It is the mother of sins. It is the appalling source of misery, pauperism, and crime. It is the source of three-fourths of all the crime, thus it is the source of three-fourths of all the taxation necessary to prosecute the criminals and care for them after they are in prison. To license such an incarnate fiend of hell is one of the blackest spots on the American Government.

"Why anti-saloon?" asks someone. "Why not anti-grocery store, anti-dry goods, anti-furniture, anti-bakery, anti-butcher shop, anti-boot and shoe store, anti-coal yard? Why single out this one business and attack that?"

"Anti-Saloon." Who is against it? The church is against it, the school is against it, the home is against it, the scientific world is against it, the railroads are against it, and every world-wide interest on earth, except the underworld, the criminal world, the immoral world and the world of crime. All cry "away with the saloon. Down with these licensed distributing centers of crime, misery and drunkenness!"

What is this traffic in rum?" "The devil in solution," said Sir Wilfred Lawson, and he was right. "Distilled damnation," said Robert Hall, and he was right. "An artist in human slaughter," said Lord Chesterfield, and he was right. "Prisoners General driving men to hell," said Wesley, and he was right. "More destructive than war, pestilence and famine," said Gladstone, he was right. "A cancer in human society, eating out its vitals and threatening its destruction," said Abraham Lincoln, he was right. "The most ruinous and degrading of all human pursuits," said Wm. McKinley, he was right. "The most criminal and artistic method of assassination ever invented by the bravos of any age or nation," said Ruskin, he was right. "The most prolific hot-beds of anarchy, vile politics, profane ribaldry and unspeakable sensuality," said Charles Parkhurst, he was right. "A public, permanent agency of degradation," said Cardinal Manning, he was right. "A business that tends to lawlessness on the part of those who conduct it and criminality on the part of those that patronize it," said Theodore Roosevelt—he was right.

"A business that tends to produce idleness, disease, pauperism and crime," said the United States Supreme Court, and it was right. "That damned stuff called alcohol," said Bob Ingersoll, and Bob was right that time sure.

Lord Chief Justice Alverstone, at the International Congress on Alcoholism, said, "after forty years at the Bar and ten years as a judge, I have no hesitancy in saying that ninety per cent of the crime is caused by strong drink."

Who foots the bills? The landlord who loses his rent, the baker, butcher, grocer, coal man, dry goods merchant whose goods the drunkard needs for himself and family, but cannot buy—the charitable people, who pity the children of drunkards, and go down in their pockets to keep them from starving—the tax payers, who are taxed to support the jails, penitentiaries, hospitals, almhouses, reformatories that this cursed business keeps filled.

Who makes the money? The brewers, distillers, saloon-keepers, who are privileged to fill the land with poverty, wretchedness, madness, crime, disease, damnation, and death, authorized by the sovereign right of the people, who vote for this infamous business.

For every $800.00 spent in producing useful and necessary commodities, the working man receives $143.50 in wages. For every $800.00 spent in producing booze, the working man receives $9.85 in wages.

The saloon comes as near being a rat hole for the working man to dump his wages in as any thing I know of.

To know what the devil will do, find out what the saloon is doing.

The man who votes for the saloon, helps the devil get his boy. The man who doesn't believe in a hell, has never seen a drunkard's home. The devil and the saloon-keeper are always pulling on the same rope.

Last year the farm products were valued at about $5,073,997,594. The brewers used $38/100$ of one per cent. The corn crop was 2,463,017,000 bushels. At 70 cents per bushel, it would

184

make $1,724,111,900. The brewers and distillers used less than 2 per cent; I will say 2 per cent, so my figures will run even. 2 per cent of 2,463,017,000 would be 49,260,340 bushels, at 70 cents a bushel would be $34,482,238. The saloon advocates cried, "if you vote out the saloons there will be a panic, the farmer will get nothing for his corn." In the past three years we have voted out of business 24,000 booze joints and the farmer receives more for his corn than ever. I believe if every saloon were voted out, it would not affect the price of corn 2 cents a bushel; furthermore, the hungry women and children of the drunkards, who have not had a square meal for years would eat up in one week the 2 per cent of corn used by the brewers and distillers in manufacturing the double distilled liquid damnation.

The entire income of the Government, to all the States and cities and towns in revenue and license was about $350,000,000. Last year the working men spent $2,290,500,000 for drink. It cost us to care for the products of the saloon, $1,200,000,000. In other words the output for the saloon, adding these amounts was $3,490,500,000. Subtract from that the income of $350,000,000; that leaves $3,140,500,000 that the saloons cost us, purely from the standpoint of cold money.

I could build 1,570,250 houses for the working people and pay $2,000 for each house with the money we spend for booze in one year. If made into $20 gold pieces and piled one on top of the other they would make a column 136 miles high. If made into silver dollars and laid side by side, they would reach 3,615 miles. If made into dimes it would be long enough to wrap a silver belt ten times around the world. In ten years I could build a silver automobile road to the moon.

The corn crop last year was $1,724,11,900 [sic]; the wheat crop last year was $878,000,000; the cotton crop last year was, $520,000,000.

We spend each year more than four cotton crops, more than three wheat crops, more than one and one-half corn crops. We are all interested in good roads. The most beautiful and picturesque highway in the United States is the Columbia Highway, carved out of the sides of Cascade Mountains, along the Columbia River, from Portland, Oregon to Hood River, a distance of about one hundred miles, but that only cost a few hundred thousand dollars.

The office of public roads in the Department of Agriculture figures the cost at $6,500 per mile to macadamize a road 16 feet wide and 7 inches thick. I will be liberal and say $25,000 for every three miles. $2,290,500,000 the amount spent for booze in one year, will build 300,000 miles of highway. Figuring the distance from New York to San Francisco at 3,000 miles, that would build 100 macadam highways. If the width of the United States from Duluth to New Orleans is 1200 miles that would build a road every twelve miles from the Atlantic to the Pacific.

The railroads are capitalized at $20,247,301,257. It would take just eight years to reproduce the railroads with the amount we spend for liquor each year.

The Treasury Department reports there are 7,581 National Banks in the United States.

Capital, $1,065,951,505.
Surplus, $726,935,755.
Total Capital and Surplus, $1,792,887,260.

Yet the money we spend for drink in the United States in one year would duplicate all the National Banks' capital and surplus and leave a balance of $700,000,000.

There are 19,240 other banks than national—that is, State and private banks.

Capital, $1,073,881,738.
Surplus, $991,147,876.
Total Capital and Surplus, $2,065,029,614.

The amount spent for drink in one year would furnish the capital and surplus and leave $400,000,000. The amount spent for drink would, in two years duplicate the capital and surplus of all the banks in the United States and leave $1,000,000,000.

The Panama Canal, perhaps the greatest engineering feat

of all time cost $400,000,000 yet we could build six Panama Canals each year with the money spent for drink. I think to license an institution that produces such misery is one of the darkest spots on our Government. I wish I could arouse every one to an uncompromising fight against the liquor traffic.

When cities get out boom editions, how many call attention to the fact that it is saloon dominated? There is no place outside the brothel, where the atmosphere is so saturated, there is no place where you can meet the filthiest characters. It is the stem around which clusters most of the infamies. The saloon unfits its owners, bartenders and patrons for the duties of citizenship. It is usually found in political alliance with keepers and supporters of gambling dives. Gambling houses and houses of prostitution are usually so closely allied with the saloon, that when the saloon is driven out, they go.

The saloon is usually found in partnership with the foes of good government. It supports the boodle alderman, corrupt law maker, the political boss and machine. It only asks to be let alone in it its law nullifying, vice and crime producing work. I have never known of a movement for good government that was not opposed by the saloon. If you believe in better civic conditions, if you believe in a greater and better city, if you believe in men going home sober, if you believe in men going to heaven instead of hell, then down with the saloon.

The liquor interests are still fat—sleek—smug and powerful with many city, state, and national governments at their feet; and they are reaching out with their slimy hands to choke, throttle and assassinate the character of those whom it cannot debauch, and who dare attack their hellish business. But their doom is sealed. If the people are fit for self government, if the people are fit for liberty, the wrath of an outraged public will never be quenched until the putrid corpse of the saloon is hanging from the gibbet of shame; praise God from whom all blessings flow.

But, says the whiskey man, "if we haven't saloons, we will lose the trade of the farmers, they will not come to town to trade, if there are no saloons." I say you lie, and by that statement you insult one of the best class of men on earth—and when you put the howl that if there are no saloons in the town the farmer won't come here to trade, why do you dump money into politics and back legislatures into the corner to prevent the enactment of county local option. The argument is often used that if you close the saloons, you thereby close the breweries and distilleries and that will bring on a panic, for it will cut off the farmer's market for his corn, and that the brewer, who furnishes him a market for his corn is his benefactor. Let us see. A farmer brings to the brewer a bushel of corn. He finds a market for it. He gets fifty cents and goes his way, with the statement of the brewer ringing in his ears that the brewer is the benefactor. But you haven't got all the factors in the problem, Mr. Brewer, and you cannot get a correct solution of a problem without all the factors in the problem. You take the farmer's bushel of corn, brewer or distiller, and you brew and distill from it four and one-half gallons of spirits. I don't know how much he dilutes them before he puts them on the market. Only the brewer, the distiller and God knows. The man who drinks it doesn't, but, if he doesn't dilute it at all, he puts on the market four and one-half gallons of intoxicating liquor—thirty six pints. I am not going to trace the thirty-six. It will take too long. But I want to trace three of them, and I will give you no imaginary stories plucked from the brain of an excited orator. I will take instances from the judicial pages of the supreme court, and the circuit court judges reports in Indiana and in Illinois to make my case.

"A few years ago in the city of Chicago, a young man of good parents, good character, one Sunday crossed the street and entered a saloon, open against the law. He found there boon companions. There was laughter, song and jest and much drinking. After awhile, drunk, insanely drunk, his money gone, he was kicked into the street. He found his way across to his mother's home. He importuned her for money to buy more drink. She refused him. He seized from the sideboard a revolver and ran out into the street and with the expressed determination

188

of entering the saloon and getting more drink, money or no money. His mother followed him into the street. She put her hand upon him in loving restraint. He struck it from him in anger and then his sister came and added her entreaty in vain. And then a neighbor, whom he knew, trusted and respected, came and put his hand on him in gentleness and friendly kindness but in an insanity of drunken rage, he raised the revolver and shot his friend dead in his blood upon the street. There was a trial; he was found guilty of murder. He was sentenced to life imprisonment and when the little mother heard the verdict—a frail little bit of a woman—she threw up her hands and fell in a swoon. In three hours she was dead.

"In the streets of Freeport, Ill., a young man of good family became involved in a controversy with a lewd woman of the town. He went, in a drunken frenzy to his father's home, armed himself with a deadly weapon and set forth in the city in search of the woman with whom he had quarreled. The first person he met upon the public square in the city, in the daylight, in a place where she had a right to be, was one of the most refined and cultured women of Freeport. She carried in her arms her babe, motherhood and babyhood, upon the streets of Freeport in the day time where they had a right to be, but this young man in his drunken insanity mistook her for the woman he sought and shot her dead upon the streets with her babe in her arms. He was tried and Judge Ferand, in sentencing him to life imprisonment, said: 'You are the seventh man in two years to be sentenced for murder while intoxicated.'

"Last spring, in the city of Anderson, you remember the tragedy in the Blake home. A young man came home intoxicated, demanding money of his mother. She refused it. He seized from the wood box a hatchet and killed his mother, and then robbed her. You remember he fled. The officers of the law pursued him, brought him back. An indictment was read to him, charging him with the murder of the mother who had given him his birth, of her who had gone down into the valley of the shadow of death to give him life, of her who had looked down into his blue eyes and thanked God for his life. And he said, 'I am guilty, I did it all.' And Judge McClure sentenced him to life imprisonment."

Now I have followed probably three of the thirty-six pints of the farmer's product of a bushel of corn and the three of them have struck down seven lives, the three boys who committed the murders, the three persons who were killed and the little mother who died of a broken heart. And now, I want to know, my farmer friend, if this has been a good commercial transaction for you? You sold a bushel of corn; you found a market; you got fifty cents; but a fraction of this product struck down seven lives, all of whom would have been consumers of your products for their life expectancy. And do you mean to say that is a good economic transaction to you? That disposes of the market question until it is answered, let no man argue further.

If ever there was a jubilee in hell it was when lager beer was invented.

I tell you, gentlemen, the American home is the dearest heritage of the people, for the people, and by the people, and when a man can go from home in the morning with the kisses of wife and children on his lips, and come back at night with an empty dinner bucket to a happy home, that man is a better man, whether white or black. Whatever takes away the comforts of home—whatever degrades that man or woman—whatever invades the sanctity of the home, is the deadliest foe to the home, to church, to state and school, and the saloon is the deadliest foe to the home, the church and the state, on top of God Almighty's dirt. And if all the combined forces of Hell should assemble in conclave, and with them all the men on earth that hate and despise God, and purity, and virtue—if all the scum of the earth could mingle with the denizens of Hell to try to think of the deadliest institution to home, to church and state, I tell you, sir, the combined hellish intelligence could not conceive of or bring forth an institution that could touch the hem of the garment of the open licensed saloon to damn the home and manhood, and womanhood and business and every other good thing on God's earth.

In the Island of Jamaica, the rats increased so that they destroyed the crops, and they introduced the mongoose, which is a species of the coon. They have three breeding seasons a year and there are twelve to fifteen in each brood, and they are deadly enemies of the rats. The result was that the rats disappeared and there was nothing more for the mongoose to feed upon, so they attacked the snakes, and the frogs, and the lizards that fed upon the insects, with the result that the insects increased and they stripped the gardens, eating up the onions and the lettuce, and then the mongoose attacked the sheep, and the cats, and the puppies, and the calves, and the geese. Now Jamaica is spending hundreds of thousands of dollars to get rid of the mongoose.

The American mongoose is the open licensed saloon. It eats the carpets off the floor, and the clothes from off your back, your money out of the bank, and it eats up character, and it goes on until at last it leaves a stranded wreck in the home, a skeleton of what was once brightness and happiness.

Like a drummer on a railroad train. There were some men playing cards, and one fellow pulled out a whiskey flask and passed it about, and when it came to the drummer he said, "No." "What," they said, "have you got on the water wagon?" and they all laughed at him. He said, "You can laugh if you want to, but I was born with an appetite for drink, and for years I have taken from five to ten glasses per day, but I was at home in Chicago not long ago, and I have a friend who has a pawn shop there. I was in there when in came a young fellow with ashen cheeks and a wild look on his face. He came up trembling, threw down a little package and said, 'Give me ten cents.' And what do you think was in that package? It was a pair of baby shoes.

"My friend said, 'No, I cannot take them.'

"But he said, 'Give me a dime, I must have a drink!'

"'No, take them back home, your baby will need them.'

"And the poor fellow said, 'My baby is dead, and I want a drink.'"

Boys, I don't blame you for the lump that comes up in your throat. There is no law, divine or human, that the saloon respects. Lincoln said, "If slavery is not wrong, nothing is wrong." I say if the saloon, with its train of disease, crime and misery is not wrong, then nothing on earth is wrong. If the fight is to be won we need men—men that will fight—the church, Catholic and Protestant, must fight it or run away, and thank God she will not run away, but fight to the last ditch.

Who works the hardest for his money, the saloon man or you?

Who has the most money Sunday morning, the saloon man or you?

The saloon comes as near being a rat hole for a wage earner to dump his wages in as anything you can find. The only interest it pays is red eyes and foul breath, and the loss of your health. You go in with money and you come out with empty pockets. You go in with character and you come out ruined. You go in with a good position and you lose it. You lose your position in the bank, or in the cab of the locomotive. And it pays nothing back but disease and damnation and gives an extra dividend in delirium tremens and a free pass to hell. And then it will let your wife be buried in the potter's field, and your children go to the asylum, and yet you walk out and say that the saloon is a good institution, when it is the dirtiest thing on earth. It hasn't one leg to stand on and has nothing to commend it to a decent man, not one thing.

"But," you say, "we will regulate it by high license." Regulate what by high license? You might as well try and regulate a powder mill in hell. Do you want to pay taxes in boys or dirty money? A man that will sell out to that dirty business I have no use for. See how absurd their arguments are! If you drink Bourbon in a saloon that pays $1,000 a year license, will it eat your stomach less than if you drink it in a saloon that pays $500 license? Is it going to have any different effect on you, whether the gang pays $500 or $1,000 license? No. It will make no difference whether you drink it over a mahogany counter or a pine counter—it will have the same effect on you; it will damn you. So there is no use talking about it.

In some insane asylums, do you know what they do? When they want to test some patient to see whether he has recovered his reason, they have a room with a faucet in it, and a cement floor, and they give the patient a mop and tell him to mop up the floor. And if he has sense enough to turn off the faucet and mop up the floor, they will parole him, but should he let the faucet run, they know that he is crazy.

Well, that is what you are trying to do. You are trying to mop it up with taxes, and insane asylums, and jails, and Keeley cures, and reformatories. The only thing to do is to shut off the source of supply.

A man was delivering a temperance address at a fair grounds and a fellow came up to him and said, "Are you the fellow that gave a talk on temperance?"

"Yes."

"Well, I think that the managers did a dirty piece of business to let you give a lecture on temperance. You have hurt my business, and my business is a legal one."

"You are right there," said the lecturer, "they did do a mean trick. I would complain to the officers." And he took up a premium list and said, "By the way, I see there is a premium of so much offered for the best horse, and cow, and butter. What business are you in?"

"I'm in the liquor business."

"Well, I don't see that they offer any premium for your business. You ought to go down and compel them to offer a premium for your business, and they ought to offer on the list $25 for the best wrecked home, $15 for the best bloated bum that you can show, and $10 for the finest specimen of a broken-hearted wife, and they ought to give $5 for the finest specimen of thieves and gamblers you can trot out. You can bring out the finest looking criminals. If you have something that is good trot it out. You ought to come in competition with the farmer, with his stock, and the fancy work and the canned fruit."

As Dr. Clinton Howard said: "I tell you that the saloon is a coward. It hides itself behind stained glass doors, and opaque windows, and sneaks its customers in at a blind door, and it keeps a sentinel to guard the door from the officers of the law, and it marks its wares with false bills of lading, and offers to ship green goods to you and marks them with the name of wholesome articles of food, so people won't know what is being sent to you. And so vile did that business get that the legislature of Indiana passed a law forbidding a saloon to ship goods without being properly labeled. And the United States Congress passed a law forbidding them to send whiskey through the mails."

I tell you it strikes in the night. It fights under cover of darkness and assassinates the characters that it cannot damn, and it lies about you. It attacks defenseless womanhood and childhood. The saloon is a coward. It is a thief, it is not an ordinary court defender that steals your money, but it robs you of manhood and leaves you in rags and takes away your friends, and it robs your family. It impoverishes your children and it brings insanity and suicide. It will take the shirt off your back and it will steal the coffin from a dead child and yank the last crust of bread out of the hand of the starving child; it will take the last bucket of coal out of your cellar, and the last cent out of your pocket, and will send you home bleary-eyed and staggering to your wife and children. It will steal the milk from the breast of the mother and leave her with nothing with which to feed her infant. It will take the virtue from your daughter. It is the dirtiest, most low-down, damnable business that ever crawled out of the pit of Hell. It is a sneak, and a thief and a coward.

It is an infidel. It has no faith in God, has no religion. It would close every church in the land. It would hang its beer signs on the abandoned altars. It would close every public school. It respects the thief and it esteems the blasphemer. It fills the prisons and the penitentiaries. It despises Heaven, hates love, scorns virtue. It tempts the passions. Its music is the song of a siren. Its sermons are a collection of lewd, vile stories. It wraps a mantle about the hope of this world and that to come. Its tables are full of the vilest literature. It is the moral clearing house for rot, and damnation, and poverty, and insanity, and it wrecks homes and blights lives today.

The saloon is a liar. It promises good cheer and sends sorrow. It promises health and causes disease. It promises prosperity and sends adversity. It promises happiness and sends misery. Yes, it sends the husband home with a lie on his lips to his wife; and the boy home with a lie on his lips to his mother; and it causes the employee to lie to his employer. It degrades. It is God's worst enemy and the devil's best friend. Seventy-five per cent of impurity comes from the grog-shop. It spares neither youth nor old age. It is waiting with a dirty blanket for the baby to crawl into this world. It lies in wait for the unborn.

It cocks the highwayman's pistol. It puts the rope in the hands of the mob. It is the anarchist of the world and its dirty red flag is dyed with the blood of women and children, and it sent the bullet through the body of Lincoln; it nerved the arm that sent the bullet through Garfield and William McKinley. Yes, it is a murderer. Every plot that was ever hatched against our flag and every anarchist plot against the government and law, was born and bred, and crawled out of the grog-ship to damn this country.

I tell you that the curse of God Almighty is on the saloon. Legislatures are legislating against it. Decent society is barring it out. The fraternal brotherhoods are knocking it out. The Masons and the Odd Fellows, and the Knights of Pythias, and the A.O.U.W., are closing their doors to the whiskey sellers. They don't want you wriggling your carcass into their lodges. Yes, sir, I tell you, the curse of God is on it. It is on the down grade. It is headed for Hell, and by the grace of God, I am going to give it a push, with a whoop, for all I know how.

We have in this country 218,000 saloons. Allowing 100 feet frontage for each saloon it would make a solid street from New York to Denver. Five million men, women and children go daily into the saloons for drink. Marching twenty miles a day, it would take them thirty days to pass a given point. Marching five abreast they would reach 590 miles. There they go, look at them!

On the first day of January 500,000 of the young men of our nation enter the grog-shops and begin a public career hellward. I will let that frightful grist grind for one year and on December 31, I will ring the bell and raise the curtain and say to the saloons, "On the first day of January I gave you 500,000 of the brain, brawn and young manhood of our land; you have had them one year. What have you to show for their 12 months in your keeping. I want them back and have come in the name of father, mother, sister, sweetheart, home, God and native land. Give me back what you have had. March them out!

I count them and 165,000 have lost their appetites, and have become muttering, blear-eyed, blubbering drunkards.

What is the music I hear? A funeral dirge. Yonder goes a funeral procession 3,000 miles long. 600,000 men die from the effects of drink each year, 80 every hour, 2,000 each day. One man leaps from a train; another will plunge into a river; another will throw his hands to his head and cry, "mother," and his life will go out like a burnt match.

Do you know of any fellow, who died young because he did not drink? Do you know of any fellow who committed suicide because he drank too much water? Do you know of any fellow who killed his wife, because he drank too much coffee? The saloon is a murder mill and a poison factory. The only difference between a high-toned saloon and a low-down saloon is that one smells bad and the other stinks.

In these days when the question of saloon or no saloon is at the fore in almost every community, one hears a good deal about what is called "personal liberty." These are fine, large, mouth-filling words and they certainly do sound first rate; but when you get right down and analyze them in the light of common old horse sense, you will discover that in their application to the present controversy they mean just about this: "Personal Liberty," is for the man who, if he has the inclination and the price, can stand up to a bar and fill his hide so full of red liquor that he is transformed for the time into an irresponsible, dangerous, evil-smelling brute. But "personal liberty" is not for his

196

patient, long-suffering wife, who has to endure with what forti-
tude she may his blows and curses; nor is it for his children who,
if they escape his insane rage are yet robbed of every known joy
and privilege of childhood, and too often grow up neglected,
uncared for and vicious as the result of their surroundings, and
the example before them; "personal liberty" is not for the sober,
industrious citizen who, from the proceeds of honest toil and
orderly living, has to pay, willingly or not, the tax bills which pile
up as the direct result of drunkenness, disorder, and poverty, the
items of which are written in the records of every police court
and poorhouse in the land; nor is "personal liberty" for the good
woman who goes abroad in the town only at the risk of being
shot down by some drink-crazed creature. This rant about "personal liberty" as an argument, has no leg to stand upon.

I stand in front of the jails and penitentiaries and count the
whiskey-made criminals. One says, "Yes, Bill, I fired the gun."
Another says, "Yes, I killed my wife." Another says, "Yes, I
murdered my friend, I am waiting for the rope or the electrical
chair." And it goes on, an endless procession. Let me summon
the wifehood, and the motherhood, and the childhood and see
the tears rain down the upturned faces. I tell you, tears are too
weak for that hellish business; tears are only brackish tide water
that well up at the bidding of some occult power.

There are 865,000 whiskey orphan children in the United
States; enough in the world to belt this globe three times around,
punctured at every fifth point by a drunkard's widow.

Like Hamilcar of old, who swore young Hannibal to eternal enmity against Rome, so I propose to perpetuate this feud
against the liquor traffic, until the white-winged dove of temperance builds her nest on the dome of the Capitol at Washington
and spreads her wings of peace, sobriety and joy over our land
and we can stand a free and sober nation and sing, "My Country
'tis of thee, sweet land of liberty, of thee I sing."

As my friend Alex Cairns says, "We are getting wise to the
con-game of the four-flushing rummies." It gives you bats in
your belfry, floating giblets, and inflammation of the gizzard,

and ingrowing coffin nails. The booze hates the trade union.
Nobody ever heard of "Union made whiskey." Even a drinking
bartender can't find a job. The railroads and steel mills and the
manufacturers say, "No job for you, if you rush the growler."
    I hold a silver dollar in my hand. Come on, we are going
to a saloon. We will go into a saloon and spend that dollar for a
quart. It takes twenty cents to make a gallon of whiskey and a
dollar to buy a quart. You say to the saloon-keeper, "Give me a
quart." I will show you, if you wait a minute, how she is burned
up. Here I am John, an old drunken bum with a wife and six
kids. (Thank God, it's all a lie.) Come on, I will go down to a
saloon and throw down my dollar. It costs twenty cents to make
a gallon of whiskey. A nickel will make a quart. My dollar will
buy a quart of booze. Who gets the nickel? The farmer, for corn
or apples. Who gets the ninety-five cents? The United States
Government, the big distillers, the big corporations. I am John,
a drunken bum, and I will spend my dollar. I have worked a
week and got my pay. I go into a grog-shop and throw down
my dollar. The saloon-keeper gets my dollar and I get a quart of
booze. Come home with me. I stagger, and reel, and spew into
my wife's presence and she says:
    "Hello, John, what did you bring home."
    "A quart."
    What will a quart do? It will burn up my happiness and
my home and fill my home with squalor and want. So there is
the dollar. The saloon-keeper has it. Here is my quart. I have
that. There you get the whiskey end of it. Here you get the
workingman's home end of the saloon.
    But come on; I will go to a store and spend the dollar for a
pair of shoes. I want them for my son, and he puts them on his
feet, and with the shoes to protect his feet, he goes out and earns
another dollar, and my dollar becomes a silver thread in the
woof and warp of happiness and joy, and the man that owns the
building gets some, and the clerk that sold the shoes gets some,
and the merchant, and the traveling man, and the wholesale
house gets some, and the factory, and the man that made the

shoes, and the man that tanned the hide, and the butcher that bought the calf, and the farmer that raised the calf, and the little colored fellow that shined the shoes, and my dollar spread itself and nobody is made worse for spending the money.

I join the Booster Club for business and prosperity. A man said: "I will tell you what is the matter with the country, it's over-production." You lie; it is under-consumption.

Say, wife, the bread that ought to be in your stomach to satisfy the craving of hunger, is down yonder in the grocery store, and your husband hasn't money enough to carry it home. The meat that ought to satisfy your hunger hangs in the butcher shop. Your husband hasn't money to buy it. The cloth for a dress is lying on a shelf in the store, but your husband hasn't the money to buy it. The whiskey gang has his money.

What is the matter with our country? I would like to do like this. I would like to see every booze-fighter get on the water wagon. I would like to summon all the drunkards in America and say: "Boys, let's cut her out and spend the money for flour, meat, and calico; what do you say?" Say!

Come on; I'm going to line up the drunkards. Everybody fall in. Come on, ready, forward, march, right, left, here I come with all the drunkards. We will line up in front of a butcher shop. The butcher says: "What do you want, a piece of neck?"

"No; how much do I owe you?"

"$3.00."

"Here's your dough. Now give me a porterhouse steak and a sirloin roast."

"Where did you get all that money?"

"Went to hear Bill and climbed on the water wagon."

"Hello! What do you want?"

"Beefsteak."

"What do you want?"

"Beefsteak."

We empty the shop and the butcher runs to the telephone. "Hey, central, give me the slaughter house. Have you got any beef, pork, and mutton?"

They strip the slaughter house and then telephone to Swift, and Armour, and Nelson Morris, and Cudahy, to send down train loads of beefsteaks.

"What's the matter?"

"The whole bunch has gotten on the water wagon!"

And the big packers in Chicago say to their salesmen: "Buy beef, pork and mutton."

The farmers see the price of cattle and sheep jump up to three times their value. Let me take the money you dump into the whiskey hole and buy beefsteak with it. I will show you what is the matter with America. I think the liquor business is the dirtiest, rottenest business this side of Hell.

Come on; are you ready? Fall in! We line up in front of a grocery store.

"What do you want?"

"Why I want flour."

"What do you want?"

"Flour."

"What do you want?"

"Flour."

"Pillsbury, Minneapolis, Sleepy Eye?"

"Yes; ship in train loads of flour; send on the fast mail schedule, with an engine in front, one behind and a Mogul in the middle."

"What's the matter?"

"Why, the workingmen have stopped spending their money for booze, and have begun to buy flour."

The big mills tell their men to buy wheat and the farmers see the price jump to over $2.00 per bushel. What's the matter with the country? Why, the whiskey gang has your money and you have an empty stomach, and yet you will walk up and vote for the dirty business.

Come on, cut out the booze, boys. Get on the water wagon; get on for the sake of your wife and babies, and hit the booze a blow.

Come on, ready, forward, march! Right, left, halt! We are in front of a dry goods store.

"What do you want?"

"Calico."

"What do you want?"

"Calico."

"What do you want?"

"Calico."

"Calico; all right, come on." The stores are stripped.

Hey, Marshall Field, Carson, Pirie, Scott & Co., J. V. Farwell, send down calico. The whole bunch has voted out the saloons and we have such a demand for calico, we don't know what to do. And the big stores telegraph to Fall River to ship calico, and the factories telegraph to buy cotton, and they tell their salesmen to buy cotton, the cotton plantation man sees cotton jump up to $150 a bale.

What is the matter? Your children are going naked and the whiskey gang has your money. That's what's the matter with you. Don't listen to those old whiskey-soaked politicians who say "stand-pat for the saloon."

Come with me. Now, remember, we have the whole bunch of booze fighters on the water wagon, and I'm going home now. Over here I was John, the drunken bum. The whiskey gang got my dollar and I got a quart. Over here I am John on the water wagon. The merchant got my dollar and I have his meat, flour and calico, and I'm going home now. "Be it ever so humble, there's no place like home, without booze."

Wife comes out and says: "Hello, John, what have you got?"

"Two porterhouse steaks, Sally."

"What's that bundle, Pa?"

"Cloth to make you a new dress, sis. Your mother had fixed the old one so often, it looks like a crazy quilt."

"And what have you there?"

"That's a pair of shoes for you, Tom; and here is some cloth

201

to make you a pair of pants. Your mother has patched the old ones so often they look like the map of the United States."

What's the matter with the country? We have been dumping the money into the whiskey hole that ought to have been spent for flour, beef and calico, and we haven't filled that hole up yet.

A man comes along and says: "Are you a drunkard?"

"Yes, I'm a drunkard."

"Where are you going?"

"I am going to Hell!"

"Why?"

"Because the Good Book says: 'No drunkard shall inherit the Kingdom of God,' so I am going to Hell."

Another man comes along and I say: "Are you a church member?"

"Yes, I am a church member."

"Where are you going?"

"I am going to Heaven."

"Did you vote for the saloon?"

"Yes!"

"Then you should go to Hell."

Say, if the man that drinks the whiskey goes to Hell, the man that votes for the saloon that sold the whiskey to him will go to Hell. If the man that drinks the whiskey goes to Hell, and the man that sold the whiskey to the men that drank it goes to Heaven, then that poor drunkard will have the right to stand on the brink of eternal damnation and put his arms around the pillar of justice, shake his fist in the face of the Almighty and say, "Unjust! Unjust!" If you vote for the dirty business you ought to go to Hell as sure as you live, and I would like to fire the furnace while you are there.

Some fellow says: "Drive the saloon out and the buildings will be empty." Which would you rather have, empty buildings, or empty jails, penitentiaries and insane asylums? You drink the stuff and what have you to say? You that vote for it, and you that sell it? Look at them painted on the canvas of your recollection.

What is the matter with this grand old country of ours? I heard my friend, George Stuart, tell how he imagined that he walked up a mill and said:

"Hello, there, what kind of a mill are you?"

"A saw mill."

"And what do you make?"

"We make boards out of logs."

"Is the finished product worth more than the raw material?"

"Yes."

"We will make laws for you. We must have lumber for houses."

He goes up to another mill and says:

"Hey, what kind of a mill are you?"

"A grist mill."

"What do you make?"

"Flour and meal out of wheat and corn."

"Is the finished product worth more than the raw material?"

"Yes."

"Then come on. We will make laws for you. We will protect you."

He goes up to another mill and says:

"What kind of a mill are you?

"A paper mill."

"What do you make paper out of?"

"Straw and rags."

"Well, we will make laws for you. We must have paper on which to write notes and mortgages."

He goes up to another mill and says:

"Hey, what kind of a mill are you?"

"A gin mill."

"I don't like the looks nor the smell of you. A gin mill; what do you make? What kind of a mill are you?

"A gin mill."

"What is your raw material?"

"The boys of America."

The gin mills of this country must have 2,000,000 boys or shut up shop. Say, walk down your streets, count the homes, and every fifth home has to furnish a boy for a drunkard. Have you furnished yours? No, then I have to furnish two to make up.

"What is your raw material?"

"American boys."

"Then I will pick the boys up and give them to you!"

A man says: "Hold on, not that boy; he is mine!"

Then I will say to you what a saloon-keeper said to me when I protested: "I am not interested in boys; to hell with your boys."

"Say, saloon, gin mill, what is your finished product?"

"Bleary-eyed, low-down, staggering men and the scum of God's dirt, that have gone to the mat and taken the count."

Go to the jails, go to the insane asylums and the penitentiaries, and the homes for feeble-minded. There you will find the finished product of their dirty business. I tell you it is the worst business this side of Hell, and you know it.

Listen! Here is an extract from the *Saturday Evening Post* of November 9th, 1907, taken from a paper read by a brewer. You will say that a man didn't say it: "It appears from these facts that the success of our business lies in the creation of appetite among the boys. Men who have formed the habit scarcely ever reform, but they, like others, will die, and unless there are recruits made to take their places, our coffers will be empty, and I recommend to you that money spent in the creation of appetite will return in dollars to your tills after the habit is formed."

What is your raw material, saloons? American boys. Say, I would not give one boy for all the distilleries and saloons this side of Hell. And they have to have 2,000,000 boys every generation. And then you tell me you are a man, when you will vote for an institution like that. What do you want to do, pay taxes in money or in boys?

I feel like an old fellow in Tennessee who made his living by catching rattle snakes. He caught one with fourteen rattles and put it in a box with a glass top. One day when he was sawing wood his little five-year-old boy, Jim, took the lid off and the rattler wriggled out and struck him in the cheek. He ran to his father and said: "The rattler has bit me." The father ran and chopped the rattler to pieces, and with his jack-knife, he cut a chunk from the boy's cheek and then sucked and sucked at the wound to draw out the poison. He looked at little Jim, watched the pupils of his eyes dilate and watched him swell to three times his normal size, watched his lips become parched and cracked, and his eyes roll, and little Jim gasped and died.

The father took him in his arms, carried him over by the side of the rattler, got on his knees and said: "Oh, God, I would not give little Jim for all the rattlers that ever crawled over the Blue Ridge Mountains."

And I would not give one boy for every dirty dollar you get from the hell-soaked liquor business or from every brewery and distillery this side of Hell.

Listen! In a northwest city a preacher sat at his breakfast table one Sunday morning. The doorbell rang, he answered it, and there stood a little boy, twelve years of age. He was on crutches, right leg off at the knee, shivering, and he said, "Please, sir, will you come up to the jail and talk and pray with papa. He murdered mamma. Papa was good and kind, but whiskey did it, and I have to support my three little sisters. I sell newspapers and black boots. Will you go up and talk and pray with papa? And will you come home and be with us when they bring him back? The governor says we can have his body after they hang him."

The preacher hurried to the jail and talked and prayed with the man. He had no knowledge of what he had done. He said: "I don't blame the law, but it breaks my heart to think that my children must be left in a cold and heartless world. Oh, sir, whiskey, whiskey did it."

The preacher was at the little hut when up drove the undertaker's wagon and they carried out the pine coffin. They led the little boy up to the coffin, he leaned over and kissed his father and sobbed, and he said to his sisters: "Come on sisters, kiss papa's cheeks before they grow cold." And the little hungry, ragged, whiskey orphans hurried to the coffin, shrieking in agony. Police, whose hearts were adamant, buried their faces in their hands and rushed from the house, and the preacher fell on his knees and lifted his clenched fist and tear-stained face and took an oath before God, and before the whiskey orphans, that he would fight the cursed business until the undertaker carried him out in his coffin.

You men now have a chance to show your manhood. Then in the name of your pure mother, in the name of your manhood, in the name of your wife and the pure, innocent children that climb up in your lap and put their arms around your neck, in the name of all that is good and noble, fight the curse. Shall you men, who hold in your hands the ballot, and in that ballot hold the destiny of womanhood and children and manhood, shall you, the sovereign power, refuse to rally in the name of defenseless men and women and native land? No!

I want every man to say: "God, you can count on me to protect my wife, my home, my mother and my children and the manhood of America."

By the mercy of God, which has given to you the unshaken and unshakable confidence of her you love, I beseech you make a fight for the women who wait tonight until the saloons spew out their husbands and their sons, and send them home maudlin, brutish, devilish, vomiting, stinking, blear-eyed, bloated-faced drunkards.

> If you knew that your boy with eyes so blue—
> With manly tread and heart so true,
> Should enter yonder bar-room bright
> And stain his soul in one wild night.
> What would you do then; what would you do?
>
> If you knew that your girl with silken hair—
> With winsome way and face so fair,
> By felon drink at last were seen
> To follow the steps of Magdalene,
> What would you do then; what would you do?

If you knew that your wife through weary years,
Should drown her grief in bitter tears,
Because her boy of tender care
Was lured to death by liquor's share;
What would you do then; what would you do?

But you know, somebody's boy must lie,
In drunken stupor and must die;
Some girl go wrong in tender years—
Somebody's wife must sob in tears
What would you do then; what would you do?

Alex Cairns

Index

Ackley, B. D., 119
Alexander, Charles M., 50
Anson, Adrian, 17-18, 19-22, 34, 76
Anti-Saloon League, 113. *See also* Prohibition
Asher, Virginia, 102-4, 134, 151-52
Asher, William, 102-4
Atlanta, Georgia, 97-98, 108, 153-54

Baltimore, Maryland, 91
Bangor, Maine, 133
Beckly, West Virginia, 133
Bellingham, Washington, 91
Bennett, Rev. Walter, 156
Bilhorn, Peter, 50
Billy Sunday Clubs, 104, 152
Bloomington, Illinois, 88
Bob Jones College, 141, 159
Boston, Massachusetts, 91, 92
Boulder, Colorado, 90, 155
Bounds, E. M., 72, 124-26, 127
    Preacher and Prayer (Power through Prayer), 125
    Satan: His Personality, Power, and Overthrow, 125, 127
Brown, Elijah P., 3, 4, 28, 48, 81, 82, 96, 98, 100, 115, 119

The Real Billy Sunday, 8, 98, 115, 119
Brown, Rev. John, 151
Bryan, William Jennings, 149, 155
Buffalo, New York, 92, 145
Business Women's Bible Clubs, 151
Businessmen's Evangelistic Clubs, 152. *See also* Billy Sunday Clubs

Canon City, Colorado, 61
Cape Girardeau, Missouri, 133
Cedar Rapids, Iowa, 90
Chapman, Rev. J. Wilbur, 49-58, 65, 72, 77, 78, 79, 86, 95, 103, 116
    Received Ye the Holy Ghost?, 57
Charlotte, North Carolina, 133, 152
Chicago, Illinois, 18-21, 23-24, 44, 50, 91, 106, 108, 115, 128, 142, 143, 144, 150
Chicago Central YMCA Bible Training Class, 28
Chicago Tribune, 122
Chicago White Stockings, 17-23, 28, 34, 37, 38, 106
Chicago World's Columbian Exposition (1893), 50
Christian Endeavor Society, 32
Cincinnati, Ohio, 126-27, 132

Cincinnati Red Stockings, 41-42, 43
Clark, Harry, 145
Clarke, Col. George R., 27
Clarke, Mrs. George R., 27-28
Cochrane, Larry, 20
Colorado Springs, Colorado, 91
Columbus, Ohio, 90, 140
Conservatism. See Fundamentalism
Coolidge, Calvin, 94, 123, 134
Corey, Martin (grandfather), 6, 13-14
Creel, George, 127

Dalrymple, A. F., 19
Dayton, Ohio, 127
Dayton, Tennessee, 148
Deeper-life movement (Keswick), 57, 72, 73, 124
Denver, Colorado, 91, 151
Denver Rescue Mission, 151, 159
Depression of 1893-94, 44
Detroit, Michigan, 92
Dickey, Rev. Sol C., 50
Dixon, Illinois, 74
Dodge City, Kansas, 133

Ellis, William T., 3, 4, 52
    "Billy Sunday": The Man and His Message, 3
Elmira, New York, 132
Emerson, Iowa, 62-63
Erie, Pennsylvania, 90
Evangelism, role in church, 46, 48-49, 50, 53
Evanston Academy, 35
Evansville, Indiana, 53, 54

Falwell, Rev. Jerry, 152
Fargo, North Dakota, 90
Farson, D. M., 118
Finney, Charles Grandison, 49, 124
    Revival Lectures, 124
Fischer, Edward, 120
Fischer, Fred, 80, 100
Fort Worth, Texas, 108
Fundamentalism, 46-47, 48-49, 51, 57, 148-49, 156-57
Fundamentalists, 46, 113

Garner, Iowa, 59, 64, 78, 79, 106
Gary, Elbert H., 127
Gault, Ontario, 53
Gibson City, Illinois, 82
Goodheart, Rev. Jim, 151

Gospel Wagon, 24
Graham, Billy, 152, 159
Grant, Ulysses S., 94, 124

Haines, Helen Sunday (daughter)
    birth of, 39
    childhood and youth of, 40, 41, 58, 83, 96, 132
    death of, 130-31
    marriage and family of, 119, 121
Haines, Mark (son-in-law), 119, 130
Haines, Paul (grandson), 130, 160
Hand Book of Iowa, A, 111
Harding, Warren G., 94, 123
Hart, Jim, 41
Henry, Carl F. H., 27
Hood River, Oregon, 95, 122
Hoover, Herbert, 134, 149-50
Howells, William Dean, 44, 85
    The Rise of Silas Lapham, 85-86
Huntingdon, Pennsylvania, 53

Indianapolis, Indiana, 53
Industrial revolution, 24, 109
Ironside, Harry, 145

Jackson, Mississippi, 132
Jacksonville, Florida, 108
Jefferson Park Presbyterian Church (Chicago, Illinois), 28, 31, 32, 77
Johnstown, Pennsylvania, 90, 118

Kansas City, Missouri, 92, 153
Kelly, Michael ("King"), 22
Keswick, England, 72
Kinney, Florence, 102

Liberalism. See Modernism
Lincoln, Abraham, 94, 124
Los Angeles, California, 95, 108, 141
Louisville, Kentucky, 132

Madisonville, Kentucky, 133
Malvern, Iowa, 63
Marquis, David C., 38
Masons, 81
Mathews, Bob, 102
Mayo, Charles, 131
Mayo Clinic, 129, 131
McAuley, Jerry, 24
McClure, J. G. K., 77
McLoughlin, William G., Jr., 3, 4
    Billy Sunday Was His Real Name, 3

Memphis, Tennessee, 133
Messer, L. W., 39, 43
Meyer, F. B., 57, 72, 124
Michaux, Rev. Solomon Lightfoot, 154
Miller, Fran, 100
Minorities, 96-98, 152-55
Mishawaka, Indiana, 142-43
Mitchell, Everett, 102
Modernism, 45-47, 48, 51, 57, 72, 80, 148-49
Monmouth, Illinois, 133
Monroe, Henry, 25, 27-28
Moody, Dwight L., 29, 49, 50, 57, 65, 75, 102, 103, 116, 124
Moody Bible Institute, 50, 102
Moody Memorial Church, 144-45
Nashville, Tennessee, 132
National League, 23, 29, 34, 40
Newport News, Virginia, 133
New York City, 91, 92, 93, 94, 105-8, 113, 115, 119, 128, 153
New York Times, 79, 93, 133-34
Niagara Falls, New York, 128
Nora (housekeeper), 100, 120, 128, 130
Norfolk, Virginia, 108

Olive Branch Rescue Mission, 46
Omaha, Nebraska, 155
Ottumwa, Iowa, 89

Pacific Garden Mission, 24-28, 46, 91, 115, 150-51, 152, 159
Palmer, Phoebe, 24
Paris, Illinois, 53, 55
Patterson, Alexander, 77
Peoria, Illinois, 53, 62
Perry, Iowa, 65
Pfeffer, Fred, 19-20
Philadelphia, Pennsylvania, 91, 92, 101, 118
Philadelphia Athletics, 40-42
Pierce, S. W., 12, 13
Pierce, Mrs. S. W., 12, 13, 25
Pittsburgh, Pennsylvania, 90-91
Pittsburgh Pirates, 23, 36-39
Portland, Oregon, 132, 133
Presbyterian Church, 75, 77, 118-19
Prohibition, 90, 112-14, 149. *See also* Billy Sunday: temperance

Red Cross, 114, 115
Redwood Falls, Minnesota, 75

Rescue missions, 24-28, 46, 140-41, 150-51, 159
Rhodes, Lula, 153-54
Richmond, Indiana, 53, 127
Richmond, Virginia, 108
Rochester, Minnesota, 129
Rockefeller, John D., Jr., 94, 105, 127-28
Rockford, Illinois, 62
Rodeheaver, Homer ("Rodey"), 101-2, 103, 104, 115, 117, 118, 134-40, 145
Twenty Years with Billy Sunday, 140
Rogers, Colonel, 41
Roosevelt, Theodore, 93, 94
Russell, R. M., 78

St. Augustine, Florida, 108
St. Louis, Missouri, 132
Salida, Colorado, 62, 64, 65
Salvation Army, 46
Sax, Grace, 100
Scopes trial, 148
Scott, Col. John, 14, 15
Scott, Mrs. John, 14, 15
Shannon, Fred A., 109-10
Sharon, Pennsylvania, 89
Sheldon, Charles, 44
Shreveport, Louisiana, 133
Siebert, Fred ("Cowboy Evangelist"), 64, 80, 82, 100
Sigourney, Iowa, 59
Simpson, A. B., 124
Sioux City, Iowa, 127
Smith, Gipsy, 124
Smith, Oswald, 141
Social Gospel Movement, 45. *See also* Modernism
South Bend, Indiana, 90
Spalding, A. G., 19, 36, 38
Spellman, Frank, 122
Spokane, Washington, 88, 89
Stead, William T., 44
Sterling, Colorado, 133
Steubenville, Ohio, 90
Stone, Timothy, 145
Sunday, Albert (brother), 6, 9, 40, 41, 43, 44
Sunday, Edward (brother), 6, 9-12
Sunday, George Marquis (son)
   birth of, 43
   childhood and youth of, 58, 83, 121
   death of, 131
   and death of sister, 130-31
   divorce of, 126, 129, 133

rebellion against parents, 119-20
Sunday, Helen Amelia Thompson
(wife)
  administrative skills of, 84, 86, 100-
  101, 104-7, 128
  and Billy's funeral and memorial
  service, 145-46, 158-59
  and birth of children, 39, 43, 81-82
  courtship and marriage of, 32-38
  and crusade staff dissension, 134-39
  death of, 160
  and death of Billy, 142-43, 158
  fame of, 89-90, 94-95, 98-100, 114-15
  and family life, 83-84, 119-22, 126,
  128-32, 159-60
  and finances, 40-41, 51-52, 90-91, 95,
  115-19, 132, 139- 40, 159
  health of, 82, 83-84, 107, 114, 128, 129,
  130
  influence of on Billy, 35-38, 76
  literary endeavors of, 100-101
  "'Ma' Sunday Speaks," 101
  Ma Sunday Still Speaks, 143
  and materialism, 87-88, 90-91, 95-96,
  98
  and media attention, 98, 99-100
  and prayer, 41-42, 52, 57, 58, 84, 158
  public speaking of, 57, 99, 104, 159
  supporting Billy's call to ministry,
  41- 42, 43
Sunday, Helen (daughter). See Haines,
  Helen Sunday
Sunday, Henrietta (daughter-in-law),
  126
Sunday, Mary Jane Corey (mother),
  6-9, 25, 40, 41, 43, 44, 89
Sunday, Paul Thompson (son)
  birth of, 81-82
  childhood and youth of, 83, 100, 120,
  121
  death of, 160
  and death of sister, 130-31
  rebellion against parents, 129
Sunday, Renee (daughter-in-law), 131
Sunday, William (father), 5-7
Sunday, William Ashley ("Billy")
  and baseball, 14-16, 17-23, 28, 34, 36-
  42, 58
  birth of, 7
  and birth of children, 39, 43, 81-82
  and blacks, 96-98, 152-54
  call to ministry, 39-42
  and Chapman, J. Wilbur, 51-58

and Chicago and Northwestern
  Railway, 38
childhood and youth of, 7-16
  in Orphans Homes, 9-13
conversion and Christian training,
  24-28
courtship of Helen and marriage, 32-
  38
critics and opposition, 80, 90-91, 95,
  115-19, 126-30, 146, 150
crusades
  big-city, 88-91
  decline of, 128, 132-41, 148-49
  early, 58-63, 79-80
  finances of, 65-66, 79-80, 89, 90-91,
  99, 115-19, 132, 137, 139
  follow-up work, 104
  organization, 100-107, 128
  results of, 74-75, 83, 89, 90-93, 107-
  9, 114-15, 135-36, 138-39, 143, 150-
  51
  staff dissension, 134-39
  use of tabernacles, 65-67, 89, 92, 97,
  104-5, 133
death of, 142-43
and deaths in family, 8, 44, 130-32
and the deeper-life movement, 57,
  72, 73, 124
education of, 10, 12-13, 14, 35
evangelistic work, early efforts, 43,
  47-49
fame of, 89-90, 93-95, 98-100, 114-15,
  139
and family life, 81-84, 119-22, 126,
  128, 129-32
film offers, 139-40
and finances, 40-41, 43-44, 51-52, 79-
  80, 89, 90-91, 95, 115-19, 122, 132,
  139-40
first evangelistic meeting, 59
and the Fundamentalist/modernist
  conflict, 46-47, 48-49, 51, 57, 148-
  49, 156-57
funeral of, 144-45
half brother Roy, 9, 13
half sister Libby, 8
health of, 129-31, 141
insecurity of, 9, 13, 36-38, 52, 75-76,
  82-84, 109
licensed and ordained to preach, 75-
  78
literary endeavors, 100-101
  Love Stories of the Bible, 101, 119

and the Marshalltown Fire Brigade, 15-16
and materialism, 87-88, 90-91, 95-96, 98
and media attention, 93, 98, 99-100, 105-6
ministering to local pastors' needs, 53
his move to Chicago, 18-19
and Northwestern University, 35, 38
and politics, 93-95, 122-23, 127-28, 149-50
and prayer, 31-32, 41-42, 43, 47, 48, 52, 57, 58, 84, 106, 125, 141
preaching and public speaking skills of, 30-31, 32, 38, 47, 53-56, 147-48
promotion of harmony among Christians, 155-56
public image, 66-69
and the Red Cross, 114, 115
release from Philadelphia Athletics, 40-42
and Roman Catholics, 80-81
sale of war bonds, 93, 113-14
and spiritual warfare, 125-26, 127, 129, 134, 139
support of his mother and brother, 40, 41, 43, 44
and temperance, 29, 34, 90, 94, 112-14, 149
theological views of, 70-74, 77
and urbanization, evils of, 109-12
and World War I, 113-14, 149
and the YMCA, 28-31, 38, 39, 41, 43-44, 48-52, 58, 78, 114, 115, 152
Sunday, William Ashley, Jr. (son)
birth of, 81
childhood and youth of, 83, 96, 100, 120, 121-22
death of, 159-60
and death of sister, 130-31
divorce of, 129, 133
rebellion against parents, 126
Sunday closing laws, 21, 23
Syracuse, New York, 92

Tabernacles, 65-67, 89, 92, 97
Tabor, Iowa, 62-63
Taft, William Howard, 94, 153
Tampa, Florida, 108
Temperance. *See* Prohibition

Terre Haute, Indiana, 53
Thielicke, Helmut, 88
Thomas, Lee, 2, 4, 142
    The Billy Sunday Story, 3
Thompson, William (father-in-law), 32, 34, 35-36, 37, 39, 42, 43
Thompson, Mrs. William (mother-in-law), 33-34, 36-37
Thompson, William (brother-in-law), 142, 143
Toledo, Ohio, 90
Toronto, Canada, 141
Torrey, Reuben A., 102, 103, 116, 124
    Gospel for Today, 124
    Talks to Men, 124
Troy, New York, 53
Tulsa, Oklahoma, 127

United States Circus Corporation, 122
Urbanization, 109-12, 146

Virginia Asher Councils, 104

Ward, Mrs. Humphrey, 44
Washington, D.C., 108
Wesley, John, 116
Wesleyan holiness movement, 72, 73
West Frankfort, Illinois, 133
West Side Ball Grounds, 28
Wheeling, West Virginia, 90
Wichita, Kansas, 153, 154
Wilkes-Barre, Pennsylvania, 90
Wilson, Woodrow, 93, 123
Winona Lake, Indiana, 50, 56-57, 86, 95, 96, 103, 109, 115, 130, 142, 159
Winona Lake Bible Conference, 104, 156
Winona Lake Christian Assembly, 159
Winston-Salem, North Carolina, 133
Wise, Rabbi Stephen, 127
Women, outreach to, 100, 103, 104
Women's Christian Temperance Union, 113
Women's suffrage, 153
Woodsmen of the World, 81
Woodstock, New York, 61

Yakima, Washington, 133
YMCA, 28-31, 38, 39, 41, 43-44, 46, 49, 50, 51-52, 58, 114, 115, 152
Youngstown, Ohio, 90